Marketing Your Sunday School

5711

JERRY WILKINS

MARKETING

YOUR

SUNDAY
SCHOOL

STRATEGIES FOR THE

2 1 *st.*

CENTURY

BROADMAN PRESS
NASHVILLE, TENNESSEE

© Copyright 1992 ● Broadman Press

All rights reserved

4260-54

ISBN: 0-8054-6054-3

Dewey Decimal Classification: 268.1

Subject Heading: SUNDAY SCHOOLS - ADMINISTRATION

Library of Congress Catalog Card Number: 91-39689

Printed in the United States of America

Scripture quotations are from the *King James Version of the Bible,* except where other-wise noted.

Library of Congress Cataloging-in-Publication Data

Wilkins, Jerry, 1945-

    Marketing your Sunday school / Jerry Wilkins.

        p. cm.

    ISBN 0-8054-6054-3

    1. Sunday schools--Marketing. 2. Sunday schools--Growth.

I. Title.

BV1523.G75W55 1992

268'.1--dc20

91-39689

CIP

Dedicated to
Ron Lewis,
church growth consultant,
and
the staff of the
State Sunday School Department
of Alabama
who gave me a vision for reaching people

Contents

Introduction

Little did I know as I attended college at the University of Alabama and later at Samford University that the principles and techniques I was learning in business school would be applied to my ministry. I began to notice about midway through my pastoral ministry that "marketing strategies" were surfacing in my work with the local church and in my attempt to reach the community around the church. About the same time, I also noticed that other churches were having success through the use of these strategies. I had recently become involved in the church-growth movement and philosophy. I had seen my ministry changed drastically by the principles of Sunday School and church growth. I had seen great results in my last two pastorates. Much of the increase resulted from the use of an aggressive marketing strategy which God blessed and used to bring the increase.

I decided to study, from my "church perspective," the techniques and principles involved in the marketing process. I reasoned that if application of some of these strategies was proving effective, then a greater application of them would prove even more effective.

For several months I researched everything I could find about the secular marketing process. I found that I had applied many of those principles to my ministry, especially the evangelistic ministry of my church. I was surprised that so many of the secular marketing principles could be applied, not only to the church, but to the Sunday School Bible study program also.

It is my intention in this book to show that aggressive application of marketing techniques and strategies will dramatically impact the unchurched community and the church, also. Some churches have been using the marketing process to a limited degree. A few churches have exercised great wisdom in their use of the marketing strategies. I believe *every church* can use the marketing principles found in this book to draw more of the unchurched into the Sunday School and the church. These principles do not take the place of the basic principles of Sunday School and church growth. They enhance those principles by giving us a more forceful way of penetrating the unchurched community.

This strategy assumes the church and the Sunday School has a quality experience to market. If the church has not exercised good "quality control" and provided quality Bible study, quality fellowship, and quality follow-up strategy; it is dangerous to "compel them in" until this is done. This is a prerequisite for any marketing strategy. In the long run, it will do more harm than good to bring people into a "negative church experience."

No matter what its size, every church can benefit from the use of these marketing methods and strategies. A small-membership church can use those strategies that require few people and little, if any, financial resources. A declining or dying church can use marketing methods and strategies to reduce losses and attract new people. The church on a plateau can begin to grow again through the use of these strategies. A growing church of any size will increase its rate of growth as these strategies are utilized.

It is important to remember two factors. First, we can do nothing without the empowering presence of Jesus. The greatest investment to be made in this process is time spent in prayer. Pray often and intensely that God would use your marketing message to convict lives. The results of all our efforts depend on the work of the Holy Spirit and God must give the increase. These strategies are the works we do that He might do His work through us. Second, if a church is full of internal problems or is unwilling to "be the church" at its best in all other areas, these strategies will not constitute a quick fix.

But, if a church is depending on the power of God and has its house in order, the ongoing use of these strategies will bring exciting results. It's worth a try . . . amen?

1

Marketing Your Best-Kept Secret

Is your Sunday School the best-kept secret in your community? Are the unchurched aware of the benefits and the values of attending your Sunday School? Think about it! Your Sunday School will help make a man a better husband and father. Have we told anyone? Your Sunday School will help a woman be a better wife and mother. But, have we told anybody? Regular attendance in your Sunday School will help children respect and appreciate their parents more. Have we told unchurched parents around your church about this benefit? Regular attendance in your Sunday School will help keep teenagers off drugs and alcohol. It will, hopefully, make them a part of the minority that abstains from immorality. But have we told anybody that?

You see, there are tremendous benefits to attending the Sunday School Bible study experience. The problem is the church has not effectively marketed the benefits and the values of the Sunday School experience. Our strategy has been to invite people to consume the Sunday School Bible study project, yet we seldom explain why. If there is value in attending Sunday School, why would we keep it a secret from the unchurched? Who in your church is charged with the responsibility of convincing the unchurched and those who do not attend Sunday School that there is value and benefit to be derived from this investment of their time?

A World in Spiritual Need

I don't need to remind you that we live in a world with spiritual needs. You're reading this book because you are sensitive to the growing number of lost and unchurched people, not only around your church, but around the world. You know, as I do, that world population is growing faster than the mind can conceive. The population around your church is probably also growing. If the population of unchurched people around your church is not growing you probably are becoming aware of the number of unchurched that already exist within the church field. One pastor for whom I was conducting a revival drove with me down one road near his church. He had explained to me that they had reached just about all of the people in their community and that their lack of numerical growth was due to the fact that there was so few prospects. He was amazed as we studied the houses up and down this road. Before we had driven two miles, we had identified twenty prospect families. We often become so familiar with our church fields that "we not see the forest for the trees." We look at our church field from such a broad perspective that we are not seeing the individual families all across the community that do not actively attend church anywhere.

A World of Change

Our world is also changing. Technology is changing so fast that even those of us who are computer literate are having trouble keeping up. The world is changing religiously. Everywhere we look, even in the smallest town, there are cults and false religions cropping up. There is upheaval everywhere as those things we thought to be solid and secure continue to change and even crumble around us.

It is a confused world. The issues that confront us in the

last few years of the twentieth century are many. The unchurched community is confused by the mixed messages being sent by so much of the Christian church. On the one hand they hear that the Bible is to be taken literally and then on the other hand that it is simply a book of suggestions, many of which are now outdated. They hear the church saying that sexual immorality is wrong in the sight of God and then they hear the church debating whether or not to condone sexual activity of any and every type. They are confused by the fallen preachers and church scandals that they have seen so widely publicized in the media. They don't understand the changes taking place, challenging those bedrock beliefs they were taught as children. We live in a confused world!

A Lost World

It is also a lost world. Recent estimates tell us approximately one third of the earth's population claims to be Christian. That leaves two thirds of the world's population either professing no religion at all or a religion we as Christians believe would not stand the test of God's judgment. Added to the tremendous number of lost in our world is the number of Christians who have forsaken the church for all practical purposes. There are thousands of people around your church that claim to be Christian but seldom, if ever, darken the doors of the church. These are two of the major groups we will address as we "market" the Sunday School.

Let me add, it is a churched world. I am excited to say that one third of the world's population professes Christianity. What an exciting day we live in! There are over one billion Christians alive on planet Earth today. They live in every nation, in every corner of the Earth. They are part of every facet of life on this planet. The church today is a mighty, massive army that could, and will with the right strategy, impact the world greatly for God. Your church can be a part of the powerful influence that God is exerting around the world today. Your church can dramatically affect the community around it.

Sunday School Remedy

The church in the world I have described above is God's channel for His caring concern for that world. I believe that the Sunday School is the most effective tool the church has for reaching a lost world. The powerful strategy of the Sunday School is simple! We bring lost and unchurched people the influence of the Word of God which will change their lives. God's Word is powerful and effective! It is used by the Holy Spirit to bring about changes that cannot be brought about in any other way. The objective of the church is to bring people in touch with the powerful written Word. So how do we get people into a Sunday School Bible study experience? I believe the answer is partially found in the pages you are about to read.

A Church Definition of Marketing

In my attempt to understand the marketing strategy in relationship to the church, I had to come up with a church definition of the marketing process. I have taken the secular marketing principles that have been shown to be so effective in the world and applied them to the church setting. It is too often said that the church is not willing to use new strategies, especially those that have been used by our world. Many would frown at the idea of selling the church or marketing the church. Yet the church doesn't have too much trouble talking about "communication," "evangelism," "witnessing," "telling," even "promoting." I believe the church has always sought to market its message and its program. We just have not done it very well in the twentieth century. So what is my church definition of marketing? *Church marketing is the sharing of the benefits of the church so that unchurched persons choose to become actively involved in the church.* I believe the Sunday School Bible study experience is the most marketable product the church possesses. In the Sunday School a person can find salvation, help for daily living, a growing personal relationship with God, fellowship with other Christians, and a deeper understanding of God's Word. Our purpose is to so market the Sunday School that persons find in it the Lord of life.

The church has readily accepted and used many modern inventions and conveniences over the last century. We use the automobile and other means of transportation. We quickly saw the need to use electricity and all of the convenience items that it has made possible. It is time we more effectively use contemporary marketing tools to share the Bible study experience. In doing so we will find the lives of thousands changed as they come under the powerful influence of God's Word.

2

The Sunday School Marketing Concept

If the Sunday School Bible study experience of your church has value and benefit, you can market your Sunday School and see more people attend. As we consider the Sunday School marketing concept, we will give attention to the entire marketing process. We will look at the product—the Bible study experience. We will define its benefits and the values derived from it. Then, we'll look at the "packaging" of the Sunday School. We will talk about product "quality control" in the Sunday School to ensure the benefits and values. We will look at all the different "target audiences." We will then explore new ways to get the Bible study experience to the consumers. We will spend much of our time looking at ways to tell non-Sunday School attenders why they should attend Sunday School.

Is This Approach Biblical?

I believe this "marketing" approach is biblical. There is no doubt in my mind that the single most effective way to win our world to Christ is for a Christian to tell another person about Jesus Christ and what He has done. You know, as I do, that if every living Christian were to win one person to faith in Christ each year, we would evangelize the world in a very short time. Since the majority of the Christian community is, for whatever reason, unwilling to adopt this strategy, we must seek alternatives methods if we are to carry out the Great Commission of our Lord. That Commission has involved many different strategies over the past two thousand years. I am suggesting that a marketing strategy revolving around the Sunday School could do much to evangelize the world. I believe Jesus "marketed" the gospel while He was on the earth. He explained the benefits of a relationship with God. He talked often of the value of knowing Him.

Think for a moment with me about just a few of the "benefits" mentioned in the Gospels alone.

Matthew:
6:11—God will meet our needs;
6:12—forgiveness of our sins;
7:13—save us from destruction, give us life;
11:28—rest from life's burdens;
28:19—purpose in life through involvement in mission of Christ.

Luke:
10:21—Treasure in heaven;
11:13—God dwelling in you;
15:1—the lost being found;
19:1—helps you straighten out your life.

John:
1:29—takes away our sin;
3:6—gives us a new beginning, fresh start;
3:16—eternal life, unconditionally;
4:10—water for our inner thirst in unending supply.

The list goes on and on. Jesus did not apologize for telling people what God would do for them, nor did He keep it a secret. He did not expect people to follow Him with nothing to gain.

The church has also been marketing itself and the gospel

down through the years. As I read the New Testament, I find that the church often explained the benefits and the values of a personal relationship with Jesus Christ. I believe the biblical mandate to share the gospel with every person on the face of the earth gives us solid foundation for involving as many people as possible in a Bible study experience. Therefore, the Sunday School is part of the biblical method of evangelizing our world, and the marketing of the Sunday School is wise stewardship of all the resources God has placed at our disposal in the twentieth century.

I am convinced that God has been involved in a marketing strategy from the very beginning. Let me put this in marketing terms. God is the source of a product that has tremendous value and benefit—a right relationship with Him. God has provided the means for us to have that product through the person of Jesus Christ. God seeks to distribute that product through the church, with branch offices and distribution points all over the face of the earth. God has priced His product. It is free! God has spoken to target consumers. He has targeted every person on the face of the earth, not willing that any should perish. God has been involved in advertising His product. He has used prophets and angels to communicate His message. He has sent His own Son, Jesus Christ, to tell the world about this wonderful product He has made available. And now He is using the church around the world to tell every person about this wonderful product. He has called and commissioned over a billion Christians to share the good news, the values, and benefits of this product. This product is a life-changing experience through Jesus Christ that brings hope, peace, joy, purpose, and, most importantly, eternal life.

I am suggesting that the church do a better job of what God began. I am suggesting that the church release more of its resources and energies into the effective accomplishing of the marketing process.

Principles that Guide Us

Let's take a moment to look at some principles that will guide us in our marketing strategy. We have learned and applied these principles to some degree to the work of the church already. Understanding these principles will help us be more committed to a marketing strategy.

The Principle of Evangelistic Imperative

We know there is a command, a biblical imperative, given to us from God. We are to evangelize the world. There is no doubt this command involves the numerical growth of the local church. Think about why the church must grow numerically. *God commands this growth.* The Commission of our Lord in Matthew 28:19 and again in the first chapter of the Book of Acts tells us to make disciples and to evangelize the world. The story Jesus tells in Luke chapter 14 teaches us that the work of the church is to, "Go into the highways and hedges and compel them to come in." The Old Testament in Deuteronomy 31:12 tells us to gather the people together, all of them, so that they might hear the word of the Lord. He makes sure to tell them to include everyone, even the stranger within the gate of the city. The church cannot obey these commandments and not grow numerically.

God's seeking nature.—The church must grow numerically because of God's seeking nature. From the Book of Genesis where God seeks Adam and Eve in the garden, to the call of Isaiah to go for God, to the demand that Jonah go for God to Nineveh, to the New Testament where Jesus states He has come "to seek and to save that which was lost" (Luke 17:10), we're reminded that God is a seeking God. God does not simply wait for us to respond. He aggressively seeks us out.

The church that has the attitude of, "they know where we are; they can come when they want to" is not expressing rightly the seeking nature of God. In Paul's Letter to the Corinthians, he explains that the church is to be ambassadors for Christ. An ambassador rightly reflects the heart and mind of the one he represents. To rightly reflect the heart and mind of God, we must seek out the lost, aggressively going to them with a word from the Lord. To wait inside the walls of our churches for lost and unchurched people to decide to come is contrary to the very nature of God. This attitude turns the church building into twentieth-century bushels under which we hide the light of the world.

God's call to harvest.—In Luke 10 we are told the harvest was plenteous but the laborers were few. We *are* admonished to pray that the Lord of the harvest would send forth more laborers into the harvest. A church cannot pray this prayer without seeking to involve itself to the fullest extent in the reaping of the harvest. This involvement will produce numerical growth. Some say that there is no harvest around their church field. My experience is I have never served in a pastorate or seen a church field that has no harvest to be brought in. I feel that we must become more sensitive to the fruit that has been left hanging on the vines. The statistics continue to tell us that 50 to 60 percent of the typical church field is unchurched. A careful study of the county where I serve revealed that only 30 percent of the population attended any one of the 250 churches on any given Sunday. In spite of this, many say there are few people to reach and that we have too many churches. I'm convinced we are overlooking the field's potential. The fruit is trying to hide from the harvesters. We must look more closely. We must be willing to "look on the fields for they are white already unto harvest" (John 4:35) and hear God's call for harvesters.

God's burdened heart.—The burden of God's heart for the lost and unchurched demands numerical growth. In 2 Peter 3:9 we're told that God is burdened for every lost soul, not willing that any should perish. In Luke 15 we're told about lost things: the lost son, the lost coin, the lost sheep. In each case there is tremendous concern expressed about lostness and the importance of finding that which is lost. Can the church really represent the God of this passage, without having a burden for the lost and unchurched of its church field? Can a church that feels this same burden not be compelled to expend itself in the pursuit of the lost? And can a church that is really doing that, do so without any numerical growth?

The biblical pattern of the church.—The New Testament church was the church that knew Jesus personally. They didn't read about Him; these were the people who knew Him—they talked to Him; they walked with Him; they knew His heartbeat. The pattern we see set in the New Testament, especially in the Book of Acts, demands the church grow numerically. Listen to the growth pattern of the early church:

Acts 2:41—"Then they that gladly received his word were baptized: and the same day there were added unto them about three thousand souls."

Acts 4:4—"Howbeit many of them which heard the word believed; and the number of the men was about five thousand."

Acts 5:14—"And believers were the more added to the Lord, multitudes of both men and women."

Acts 5:28—"Did we not straitly command you that you should not teach in this name? And behold you have filled Jerusalem with your doctrine."

Acts 6:1—"And in those days when the number of disciples was multiplied."

Acts 6:7—"And the word of God increased; and the number of the disciples multiplied in Jerusalem greatly, and a great number of the priests were obedient to the faith."

Acts 8:4—"Therefore they that were scattered abroad went everywhere preaching the word."

Acts 16:20—"These men, being Jews, do exceedingly trouble our city."

Acts 17:6—"These that have turned to the world upside down are come hither also."

The early church was obsessed with reaching people and with numerical growth. We should seek to be true to our heritage and seek to grow numerically as well.

For all these reasons, and more, I believe that every church should grow numerically. To minimize the importance of numerical growth cuts the heart out of the mission of the church. To minimize numerical growth deprives God of the resources and energies of the very institution He placed upon the earth to bring people to Him. To minimize the importance of numerical growth minimizes the importance of lifting up Jesus so He might draw all people unto Him. We must continue to believe in the principle of evangelistic imperative.

Principle of Church Growth Through Sunday School

I have become convinced over the last fifteen years of my ministry that the most powerful tool available to the church is the Sunday School Bible study experience. I believe no other program in the church can do as much to reach people. In my opinion, marketing the Sunday School experience would do much to draw people into life-changing Bible study. It is for that reason that I suggest that we not only market the church and the gospel, but that we market the Sunday School. The content of our advertising strategy will

be the Sunday School Bible study experience and its benefits. If the Sunday School grows, so will every aspect of the
church. Some voices today tell us that the Sunday School
has seen its best days and will not reach people in the future.
I disagree! The Sunday School has seen its best days only if it
ceases to adapt itself to the needs of each new generation. I
believe the Sunday School will adapt to reach and teach the
masses of this world. Bible study is basic to the mission of
the church and the Sunday School is the church organized to
do this work from an evangelistic perspective.

The Principle of Seed Sowing

We have long believed in the principle that Paul taught us
in 1 Corinthians 3:6-8. Winning people to Christ is a process.
Someone must plant the seed, someone else may water the
seed and eventually God will bring the harvest. That process
may include planting, watering, weeding, fertilizing, nurtur-
ing, and eventually God will bring the increase. For that reason, we must not expect evangelism to be a one-time effort.
We must realize that winning people to faith in Christ is a
process the church must be involved in. The church must be
willing to invest enough of its time and resources so that all
facets of the process can continually go on. A marketing
strategy keeps in mind this important principle. When we
talk about "multiple contacts" and the "Godward journey,"
we will realize the marketing process is a seed-sowing and
reaping process. The lights went on for me when I was
taught for the first time that "reaching people" was a "process" that takes time, no matter what program you are using.

The Principle of Multiple Contacts

We have realized that people are not usually won to
Christ on the initial contact. Between thirteen and twenty

contacts are needed with unchurched persons to bring a favorable response about the church or Jesus Christ. The Receptivity Scale tells us that there are times when people are more open to changing their life-style. People are most open to a change of life-style (from not going to church to going to church) in the following settings:

- Times of Death (spouse, family member, friend)
- Times of Loss (divorce, separation, injury, jail)
- Times of Change (retirement, marriage, move)
- Times of Blessing (new job, children, raise)
- Times of Failure (job, financial, relationships)

If we are to touch the lives of people during the times they are more receptive to life-changing decisions, we must make multiple contacts with them, lest we miss them at those times they are most receptive. It is my contention that no fewer than four contacts must be made with every prospect each year. This is a minimum and can seldom be accomplished by the regular visitation program in the typical church. It can be accomplished through an aggressive marketing strategy using the numerous means available to us today.

The Principle of the Godward Journey

We understand that a person's decision to accept Christ does not happen overnight. Even Paul's conversion was a process, a journey toward God. Paul heard the teachings of Jesus and watched the stoning of the first Christian martyr. These experiences, no doubt, had a powerful impact on him. His dramatic conversion was the culmination of a Godward journey. Most people are somewhere on a scale from being very close to God to not even believing that God exists. Bringing people to Christ is a process of moving them toward the experience. The process of multiple contacts and an aggressive marketing strategy seeks to move people forward in their journey toward God, again and again, until they come to the place where they can express faith in Christ. Moving a person often enough to bring him to faith in Christ cannot be done by the typical visitation program. It can be done by an aggressive marketing strategy that touches people over and over again, moving them each time one step further in their Godward journey.

The Principle of Perception

Perception is how people see the church. It is important that we think about this principle from two perspectives. First, we must consider how the unchurched person perceives the church. Second, we must consider how the church perceives itself.

First, the way unchurched people see the church may be, in many ways, faulty and distorted. Their perception of the church may be distorted by what they see in the media, what they hear from others, and even what they have experienced in the past themselves. These misconceptions cause the unchurched to respond negatively to the church and its message. Many unchurched people do not attend a local church because of the way they perceive the church itself. An aggressive marketing strategy can help improve the perception or the image of the church.

An example of this is the perception change that has been brought about through the use of the media by the Mormon Church. Their example should challenge us to do a better job of presenting our image well in the media. Every local church can use an aggressive marketing strategy to improve the way people perceive the church.

Second, we must admit that how a church perceives itself affects its growth. I noticed as I applied the marketing strategy in churches where I was pastor, the church began to perceive itself as more evangelistic and as more successful. This improvement of self-image caused more people to be involved in growth activities of the church and caused the church itself to become more evangelistic in its budget and ministries.

The Principle of Cooperation

Cooperation enhances the effectiveness of any group. We can do more together than any one of us can do alone. It is true that the "whole" of cooperation will be greater than the "sum of the parts" of independent activity. What we can do together far exceeds what all of us can do alone. Denominational groups such as societies, conventions, and associations can be involved in the marketing strategy. These cooperative groups have at their disposal vast resources that can be used in the marketing strategy. The larger cooperative group can market the Sunday School and the church for a number of smaller groups or churches. Conventions, associations, societies, and other groups in the Christian context would do well to set up and fund programs that will market for all of its churches the Sunday School program. Combining resources will make it possible to use the more expensive methods of marketing advertising. Conceivably, a group of churches in a given area might combine their resources to market their Sunday School programs in that particular area. Combining resources will make it possible to multiply the number of contacts through the marketing strategy and make use of the more expensive advertising tools available to the church today.

Each church should analyze its marketing strategy. It should decide if its strategy is sufficient to draw the unchurched into its Bible-study program. Most churches can improve their marketing skills. The next chapters will discuss those skills.

3

The Process of Marketing Your Sunday School

The process of marketing your Sunday School program is on one hand—simple, and on the other hand—complex. It's simple because *marketing*, in its purest form, is the process of producing a product that meets the needs of and is consumed by consumers. It is complex because it involves product development and design, packaging, price, benefits, target audiences, distribution, advertising, and research of both market potential and consumer response. All these marketing components can be seen in the work of the church if we look at the church's evangelistic activity through "marketing eyes."

The Price of the Sunday School Product

We may feel that the Sunday School is "free" to those that attend. We may feel that the unchurched have nothing to lose—no price to pay for attending Sunday School. We forget the price we pay to attend Sunday School ourselves. Understanding the "price" of our product may help us realize the need to communicate the benefits more clearly.

Let's think about it for a minute. In order to attend, we must get out of bed on possibly the only day we could have slept late, go through the hassle of getting the children up, get "all dressed up," drive several miles, sacrifice those precious Sunday hours, and say "no" to all the other activities that beckon us.

Tell the unchurched that it costs nothing and watch the expression on their faces. Tell them there's no price they must pay, and they will tell you how little you know about their lives. We must assume they know the price, but let's not assume they know the benefits. They are very sensitive to the price they must pay if they become involved in the Sunday School or in church itself. They know it means a change of Sunday habits, expenditure of time and energy, and adjustment to unfamiliar surroundings.

We must show that the "product" is well worth the "price." My barber put a sign on his wall when he went up on the price of my haircut. It said, "IT'S NOT WHAT IT COSTS; IT'S WHAT IT'S WORTH." People will pay the price to attend the Sunday School when they are convinced of the worth of it! You do, don't you?

The Sunday School Product

Keep in mind this important fact—the church has always been involved in the marketing process, even if it has not recognized it. We have called it evangelism, promotion, communication, enlargement, or some other term. The church has a product. You might say the church *is* a product. We hope that billions of people will see, with spiritual eyes, the value of this product and partake of it personally—"consume" it. It may be that the church has not yet understood the tools now at its disposal to present what it has to offer from God to the world.

The church offers a great "product!" That product includes eternal life, hope, joy, purpose, peace, wisdom, encouragement, stability in crisis, and on and on the list goes.

All these benefits can be found as a person attends the Sunday School and the life-changing Bible study it offers. If people become involved in the Bible-study program, they become the recipients of tremendous blessings and benefits. Right? The question is, "Have we told them?" When have we really explained the benefits and values of being involved in Sunday School? We may be pushing the product without presenting the reasons "why" anyone would want our product.

Benefits of the Sunday School Product

Our goal is to convince people to be involved in the Sunday School. There they will discover the love of God and the help they need for daily living. We must convey to them the value and the benefits derived from that involvement. It is not enough to tell people that they ought to attend Sunday School. It is not feasible to expect people to attend out of a sense of guilt. We are told and can observe easily that people today are not motivated by guilt. It may be that everyone is perceived as being guilty, from the highest seats of government to the television pulpit. So being guilty does not discourage or motivate. People must be clearly and repeatedly shown the benefits and values of an activity rather than condemned for neglect of that activity. Ad suggestions later in this book will be geared to this approach. They must be clearly and repeatedly shown the benefits.

When I asked a large group of conference participants to describe the Sunday School, the descriptions showed we most often see the Sunday School through our "churched" eyes. Some of the terms included,

- Bible teaching
- outreach
- small groups

- Bible study
- fellowship
- evangelism

These terms and others identified the Sunday School from the perspective of those who were already involved. I then asked them to describe the Sunday School in terms of "benefits" to those who attended. After some thoughtful silence, they began to verbalize their newly acquired perspective. This time the terms were different. They began to share terms like:

- understanding the Bible
- caring fellowship
- knowing God's will
- friendship
- learning how to live forever
- finding purpose in life
- better marriages
- encouragement
- improved family life

On and on they went, and we discovered together that our Sunday School product had many benefits we had never shared with our potential consumers. Most of those present admitted that we are keeping the "benefits" of the Sunday School as our "best-kept secret." We fail to tell people "why" they should be involved in our Sunday School. An important part of the marketing process is the development of a beneficial product. We have that product: Sunday School!

We must educate our members to think in these terms and to share these benefits as they seek to reach people. We must see the Sunday School in terms of the benefits it provides.

We must use every possible means to communicate these benefits to the people around our churches and around our world.

Packaging the Sunday School Product

"Packaging" any product is vital. Companies spend millions on the "packaging" aspect of the marketing process. These companies research what people respond to, what size box they like, what color and layout attracts attention, and what different images bring to a person's mind. They will even put the same product, with some slight variation, into different packages to attract different customers. A wise fisherman uses several different sizes and colors of artificial worms in an attempt to find which one the fish are attracted to at any given time.

A church would do well to give greater consideration to "packaging" the Sunday School experience. Consider for a moment the building where your Sunday School meets. It should be attractive and well maintained. It should be well lighted and have an atmosphere of warmth and acceptance. The grass should be cut; the parking should be adequate, including paving, well-marked visitors' spaces, and striping so that cars are not crowded. (People who pay $10-20,000 for a car care about this!) Count your parking spaces. You should provide one space for every 2.5 people who attend or, better put, whom you want to attend your Sunday School and church. (Don't forget high-attendance days.)

Remember this accepted rule of thumb: If you are 80 percent full, you are *full!* Check your parking this Sunday. How many spaces do you have left for those you hope will come? One pastor told me he planned to reach one-hundred more people in the coming year. After looking over his church, I asked him how he planned to get thirty or forty more cars into the three parking spaces he had left? Don't wait until you are out of parking spaces to plan more. It will take several months, at best, to provide the needed new spaces.

The building entrances should be well marked, and greeters should be on hand to assist newcomers. I've talked to several people who were drawn to a church because that church took the time to mark the visitor's entrance. One man said he went to three churches one morning before he found one that told him which door to enter. (It seemed to be important to him!)

The inside of the Sunday School building—remember, your building *is* your package—should be clean and well maintained. This is especially true of classrooms. "Welcome" signs should assure newcomers that they are welcome and, of course, expected. These "Welcome" signs can be located in the hallways and the classrooms, as well as the entrances. Chairs should always be available and free of dust, rusty sharp edges, and dead crickets or spiders. Extra pieces of Sunday School literature should be close at hand for the newcomer; and free copies of your textbook—the Bible—should be given whenever a visitor comes without one. Expensive, you say? What's a soul worth to your church? (As much as the new bus, or the new pads on your pews, or that new organ?)

If it seems a little picky to deal with such matters as the building; be advised that recent surveys reveal that one of the top reasons listed by the unchurched for not attending was that the building, especially the nursery, was dirty. It may be that people have come a long way in what they expect in the way of clean homes, businesses, and churches. It behooves us to check our "packaging"—our classrooms, our hallways, our restrooms, and, for sure, our nurseries. We would do well to use some of our Lord's financial resources to purchase signs to help newcomers find their way around. One man in a conference I conducted told the group, "The only signs in our church are those telling folks how to get out!"

Many churches realize that an important part of the packaging is the "people" of the church. They teach the church how to be accepting and friendly. Ushers, greeters, and welcome committees are trained to roll out the red carpet for newcomers. I can remember as a pastor training my ushers to seat newcomers in certain areas of the sanctuary as opposed to other areas. It was part of our churchwide strategy to make sure our visitors got the best possible reception. Welcome centers are becoming commonplace, and visitor buttons are used to identify newcomers so members can make a special effort to greet them. Some surveys imply visitors do not want to be singled out, but I believe it can be effective if done tactfully. There is no substitute for a friendly smile and a warm "I'm glad you're here."

What About Alternative Packaging?

The Sunday School product, with all these benefits, might be consumed by more people if it were offered in a variety of packages. An ever-growing number of people cannot attend at the traditional place or the traditional time. Still others will not! While continuing to offer the Sunday School Bible-study experience in the church building at the Sunday-time, class-type package, the church should consider a variety of packaging options.

Many churches now offer Sunday School outside the church building. Classes are being held in apartment complexes, fire stations, storefronts, senior citizens groups, and in homes. The possibilities are unlimited—restricted only by our lack of creativity.

In an effort to reach those who cannot be drawn into traditional classes, "cassette classes" are being offered to some who spend large amounts of time commuting to work. It is possible that this type class will be effective in reaching people who are hindered somewhat by "shyness," a speech handicap such as "stuttering," for example. We have all heard of taping the sermon for the homebound; why not tie them to a Sunday School class through this tool?

Our alternative packaging can utilize special Bible-study materials. Many of these materials are now available. Special materials are being used to draw people into the Sunday School experience. These special classes, sometimes four to eight weeks long, attempt to "scratch where they itch." For example, classes can be offered for people who are new church members, who are about to be married or just married, those who are adjusting to recent loss of a loved one, and those learning how to care for that first baby. It may be that the Sunday School of the future will be "menu driven." People will be offered several choices as they enter the Bible-study arena. These classes will apply Bible to current issues and include such areas as environment, home and family improvement, health, and so forth. As I wrote these lines, my eighteen-year-old daughter and her boyfriend came through the room. I told them of my vision of a future church and how it might be different in this area. They stopped to listen (that was a miracle in itself) and expressed excitement and enthusiasm at the thought of such a church.

It makes sense! Today, people are offered choices at every turn, at every decision, at every juncture of life. Yet, when they come to church, we offer them one choice. (Is that really a choice at all?) They turn on the television and have dozens of choices as to which channel they will watch. We are told that 13,000 new products appeared on grocery shelves this past year. One hundred and twenty-three new cereal products were unveiled in 1990 alone. The average grocery store gives us the choice of more than 17,000 products. Movie theaters now offer six to ten movies to choose from on a single night. At the magazine stand, we see hundreds of choices with dozens in any subject area. Get the point! They get choices everywhere but at church. One time, one place, one subject! It's "have it *our* way" at the local church. The church needs to roll up its sleeves and do the hard work of offering the "good news" in a variety of packages.

These classes of different subjects, different times, and different places become "ports of entry" where people enter the Sunday School, the church, and, eventually, the Christian faith. Details of these classes will be discussed in the chapter on "marketing tools."

Our evaluation of "packaging" will lead us to consider using the term "Bible study" and "Sunday School" when we are seeking to reach unchurched adults, especially men. Some people still think "Sunday School" is for children. Alternate terms can overcome some of the resistance we experience. Using "Bible learning" or "Bible discovery" or even "Bible search" rather than "study" or "class" might be better. I'm sure teenagers do not get excited about more "class," more "lessons," and more "study" after a week of the same at school. These alternate terms sound strange, even to me—just like those we use today did when we first used them. Surely there are terms we can discover and use that will be more attractive to the unchurched (and to our active people also).

I am convinced there are ways to package the Sunday School that are "yet to be discovered." It is sad that so many of those that have been discovered are still not being utilized by so many of our churches. Large numbers of people can be reached by churches who use these and other innovative approaches. A great day will have dawned when more churches begin to offer the Sunday School experience in different places, on different days, at different times, and with different choices as to content. Great days are ahead for churches who give innovative attention to the "packaging" aspect of the marketing process.

Target Audiences for the Sunday School

Another component of the marketing process is the targeting of different audiences, different groups of people your church wishes to "compel in." In our enthusiasm to reach "everyone," we may have targeted "no one." The shotgun approach does not take into consideration different human needs, attitudes, and tastes. Ask this question, "Whom do we want to reach?" What group of people do you wish to influence at this time? How should you market the Sunday School in order to reach each group of people that live within the ministry range of your church? These questions need to be answered by every church.

Let's look at these broad target audiences: The unchurched non-Christian, the inactive Christian, the non-Sunday School church member, the inactive Sunday School member, and the active-now Sunday School member.

In addition, each of these groups can be broken down into subgroups as to age, marital status, special needs, etc. Each target group can be addressed in a different way. The promotional channel you choose will be determined by which group you have targeted.

The Unchurched Non-Christian

The unchurched non-Christian continues to make up a large segment of every church field. These people are defined as those who have not become Christians and do not attend church anywhere. Reaching this group means speaking in a "language" they understand. We must think from their perspective. In one of my pastorates, I remember a public relations committee struggling for hours choosing words that would better communicate with unchurched non-Christians. They realized that our "church lingo" would not do.

Addressing this target audience will also require skillful use of the available communication tools. They do not read the church page nor do they give their attention to ads for "revival" or other "church-type" activities. They usually tune out those things which include "churchy images." If we are to be effective in reaching the unchurched non-Christian, we must pay attention to our content, our artwork, and our choice of media. We will look closer at this in a later chapter. Let's look at another audience.

Inactive Christians

Inactive Christian may seem like a contradiction of terms. Yet, there are millions of people who say they are Christians but never attend church or Sunday School. Many of them resent being identified as "unchurched" because their names are on a church roll somewhere. Recent survey[1] results tell us that more than half of the unchurched adults in America say they believe in Jesus, have a Bible in their home, and have made some kind of commitment to Jesus in the past. The debate over the genuineness of their commitment should not keep us neutralized in our effort to reach them for active church life or for a genuine conversion experience, whichever the case may be. We must convince them of the benefits of active involvement in a Bible-study program and in church itself.

In many cases, our task is to move them from "head knowledge" to "heart commitment." In other cases, it is to lead them to rekindle a faith that somehow was smothered in the past. Addressing this group will also require great creativity and wisdom. We must "think like they think." Packaging and content of our promotion must be tailored to speak to them "where they are." We might do well to ask the simple question, "What would it take to draw me in if I were an inactive Christian?" Let's consider yet another target audience.

Non-Sunday School Church Members

The non-Sunday School church member attends worship but never Sunday School. Every church has members like this. How many does your church have?

Why spend time, effort, and even money getting these people into Sunday School? Let's think for a moment. Our first motive springs out of the reason for this book: *People need Sunday School!* They will benefit greatly by being in Sunday School, and we want them to receive all these benefits. A second motive is the fact that a church member who is active in Sunday School will pray more, give more, and serve the Lord and His church more. There are exceptions to this rule, but wouldn't your church benefit greatly if this group became active in the Sunday School?

This group is a great target audience for our marketing strategy because they are already "dressed and on the grounds." We simply must sell them on the benefits of coming one hour earlier or taking advantage of some of our alternative Sunday School packaging. The communication channels which address this audience are more numerous because we can add our "in-house" channels (pulpit, weekly newsletter, Sunday bulletin, hallways, and bulletin boards). We will examine these in a later chapter. Now let's consider our fourth target group.

Inactive Sunday School Members

Inactive Sunday School members are those folks who are on your Sunday School roll but seldom if ever attend. We could include those who attend spasmodically. These people drop in every third or fourth Sunday. In the average church, this target audience consists of more than 50 percent of the Sunday School enrollment. It has been estimated that a concentrated effort could reach one out of three in this target audience. I believe an aggressive marketing strategy that targets this group can prove successful. This group can also be addressed through "in- house" channels as well as those outside. Our strategy and the content of the message to reach this group will be somewhat different also.

Active Sunday School Members

Finally, there are those active Sunday School members. Why do I suggest we market the Sunday School to this target audience? For the same reason the Coca-Cola Company spends millions telling Coke consumers how great their product is—to keep them coming back for more. We know that we lose many active Sunday School members each year. If we could see into the spiritual lives of our active members, we would see that many are only a few steps from "dropping out." Many attend only out of "habit" or "a sense of guilt." As soon as the habit is broken by some "more attractive habit" or they learn to live with the guilt, they will be gone. A strong marketing strategy will ensure their continued attendance by giving them the *best of all reasons:* Sunday School meets their needs.

After looking at these broad target groups you will want to break them down even further in order to be very specific in your content and strategy. This will help you determine specific wording, what benefits to advertise, and which channels of communication should be used. Some of these particular groupings would include singles, teenagers, senior citizens, homebound, handicapped, baby boomers or busters, parents, the shy, and many more. The recognition of these specific target groups will affect how you word your promotion, where you place your ads, what time you do your advertising, and even who does the talking for you. It will be worth the effort to select your target audience because failing to do so may allow us to "say the wrong thing to the wrong people at the wrong time in the wrong place and in the wrong way." So take the time to choose your target audience well. Take good aim—you might just hit the "bull's-eye."

A Process Approach

Notice: all these components make up one great process. We must not expect overnight results. We must expect it to take time. It is important to realize that results come only if you begin the process and stay with it. Some results may be seen immediately, but the real results will come in the months and years ahead, and the results will be cumulative. Any church can do a better job of "marketing" the Sunday School if they give attention to these important aspects of the marketing process and trust the results to the One who gives the increase. Now, let's turn our attention to *organizing* your church for the Sunday School marketing process.

Note

1. *The Unchurched American, Ten Years Later.* Gallup Poll, 1988. (An update of *The Unchurched American,* 1978, Gallup Poll Organization.)

4

Organizing Your Church to Market the Sunday School

To begin or enhance your marketing strategy, your church must begin where it is in this process. Many churches may be doing things that would be considered "marketing" the church, but few are marketing the Sunday School experience. Let's assume that your church needs to organize itself to market the Sunday School.

Most churches are not organized to do marketing, public relations, or advertising. I find that in most cases any marketing strategy being carried out is done by the pastor, or in some cases, the educational director of the church. It is important to remember that these individuals are already overloaded and that often this most important strategy simply does not get the attention it deserves. I believe that the pastor, educational director, and other staff should be intimately involved in the marketing strategy. They should work with any director, committee, or team that is responsible for developing and implementing a marketing strategy for the Sunday School. It is essential that a church build into its organizational structure a "marketing team." I find that most initial efforts at marketing the church or the Sunday School fizzle out after only a few months. Someone other than the pastor and/or other staff must be responsible and accountable for this work. At the same time, the pastor or some other staff member must be there to motivate and inspire the team to plan and implement a strategy.

Once the church has decided to improve its marketing skills and develop a marketing strategy, the next step is to make some person or group responsible for designing and implementing the marketing strategy. As I said, the pastor and church staff should be involved with this individual or group as it develops the strategy. Pastor and selected staff should serve as "advisors" of any group which will tackle the design of this process. Staff members should share ideas and inspire the group. They should give guidance to the development of the strategy and share input out of their vision for the future of the church. Several options for making someone responsible are available to the church.

Public Relations Committee

In some churches the responsible group is called the public relations committee. There are guidelines and resources available for this type committee from several different sources. The Sunday School Board of the Southern Baptist Convention and most Baptist state conventions, for example, provide assistance for public relations committees. Denominational agencies can be most helpful in the development of a public relations strategy. If the church decides to function through the use of a public relations committee, that committee must be trained to market the Bible study program of the church. That committee must be taught to emphasize the principles that I will be presenting in the book, especially in the area of content. Too often public relations committees in churches have spent a lot of money saying the wrong thing. We tend to promote programs and features of the church rather than the benefits and values derived from participating in the church. Training is essential!

A Sunday School Marketing Director

Another option to make someone responsible for the marketing strategy is to elect a Sunday School marketing director. A church could also consider electing an assistant Sunday School director whose main responsibility will be the marketing of the Sunday School. I believe the Sunday School organization should be expanded to include not only a Sunday School director, but several assistant directors in charge of specific areas. Those areas could include enlistment and training, literature management, and the marketing strategy. In too many cases, one Sunday School director is expected to do everything. It simply is not working in most churches and much of the most important work is being neglected.

A Sunday School Marketing Committee

Another option would be to elect a Sunday School marketing committee or team. This committee would function much the same as a PR committee but would have as its central focus the marketing of the Sunday School itself. These individuals would work closely with the church staff and the Sunday School director. They would channel financial resources and energy into marketing the Bible study experience.

Choosing the Right People

What type persons should a church place in the above positions? I believe these persons should exhibit a burden for the lost and unchurched of the community. I think there should be a deep concern that the unchurched be compelled to come in. They should love all kinds of people. This committee or team can challenge the church to open its doors and its hearts to all the different kinds of people living in the ministry range of the church. These individuals should be spiritually mature and able to interact in the committee setting. They must not be domineering or nearsighted. They must not be narrow-minded and therefore unable to accept ideas from others on the team. These people must be progressive in their thinking about the work of the church. They should not be hindered by tradition and constantly resist new ideas.

They do not have to be media experts. In some cases, churches have attempted to place on the public-relations committee persons who work in radio, television, newspaper, or other areas. Although this could work, too often media professionals overemphasize their particular medium to the neglect of others. There must be a balance in the strategy and it is only natural that someone working in a particular area would be biased toward the effectiveness of that medium. It might be wiser to build the committee or team out of persons who are of the qualities above and call in for consultation persons who have expertise in different media areas.

Again, the important message of this chapter is that someone must be responsible! Someone must be accountable! If a church fails to make someone responsible for the development and implementation of a marketing strategy, the probability of failure is high. The program will be short-lived and the strategy will not have time to produce results.

Planning the Annual Strategy

The first step in planning an annual strategy is to plan the training of the person or group in charge of the marketing strategy. It does not seem feasible to give people a task without training them to do it. This training can be acquired in several different ways. Team members should purchase books about the church marketing process. There are also

47

training resources available through denominational agencies. Some individuals have given their lives to the training of groups in the marketing of the church. Denominational agencies are aware of their names and can put a church in contact with them. Many of these people will come to the church and provide training for both the committee and church.

The second step in the planning of an annual strategy is to study the community around the church. Decisions should be made about the church's ministry range, and a study of the population within this range should be completed before a strategy is developed. Demographic studies can be secured through denominational agencies and community resources The committee or team should look at the type of persons in the ministry range of the church. They should give specific attention to age, marital status, race, and religious background. Consideration should also be given to economic and educational levels. This study should be summarized in a report that will help the committee "think with the mind of the unchurched." This report can also be shared with the church at large to help it better understand its community and, more importantly, the strategy being implemented by the committee.

The next step in planning an annual marketing strategy is to look at the resources and the options available to the church. In the study of the community, the committee or team should look for all possible resources for its media strategy. Does the community have a local newspaper? Is that paper a weekly or daily? How many subscribers does the newspaper have and what percentage of the community does it touch? Are there local radio stations? What stations do most of the people in your area listen to? Can different target audiences be touched by the use of different stations?

These same questions should be asked about television stations. The committee should investigate cable systems and how could they be used to market the Sunday School. In our chapter on marketing tools, we will mention several other resources the church committee or team should be aware of. Many of these will be found in the church itself.

Providing Funds for the Marketing Process

As the marketing team looks at its resources, a primary concern will be the availability of funds for the marketing process. Most churches have little if any funds budgeted for marketing. In most cases, I find that any funds budgeted or allocated for marketing are spent in advertising revivals, homecomings, Vacation Bible School, or other events that do not attract the unchurched. In most cases, churches spend from zero to 2 percent of their total at-home expenditures in a marketing strategy designed to compel people to come in. Imagine that! Thousands, even millions of dollars are spent on buildings, maintenance, and programs and events within those buildings, yet only a very small percentage, if any, is spent on promoting and communicating the values and benefits to persons participating in these programs and events. Too often, what little money spent is spent promoting programs and features rather than the benefits and values connected with these programs.

A church should start where it is with the financing of a marketing strategy. If the church has no monies allocated toward a marketing strategy, it should begin by budgeting a small amount. This sum should be increased every year until a healthy percentage of the church's budget is being spent on compelling people to come in. This might mean that a small church would allocate two to three hundred dollars the first year and increase the amount by several hundred each year until they are spending two to three thousand dollars per year on this process. Larger churches could begin by placing in excess of a thousand dollars and increasing that amount by a healthy percentage each year. Remember, a good goal for your advertising and marketing expenditures would be 10 percent of your "at-home" expenditures. If a church adds to its budget each year for five or six years, it will find itself spending a healthy amount on its marketing strategy by the end of that period.

Remember, it is important to spend all the church allows in the annual budget. In one marketing seminar, an educational director shared with the group that he now realized that his church had allocated in excess of five hundred dollars for him to use in the promotion of his Sunday School. However, he had forgotten that this money was allocated and had failed to use it during the year. He had lost his opportunity to market his Sunday School program and to have that amount increased the following year. Don't let that happen to you!

Organizing your church is essential to the overall process. Remember, if someone is not responsible, the work will probably go undone or be short-lived. If your church does not plan a strategy, you will probably do what you had planned to do: nothing. I suggest planning a yearlong calendar of marketing activities. An example of this type calendar might read:

October: Door knockers with Sunday School testimonies.

November: Use of bulletin boards to display the benefits of Sunday School involvement.

December: Mail Sunday School quarterly to all prospects as a Christmas gift.

January: Four-part series in church mailout on the value of attending Sunday School.

Begin preparation of March direct-mail piece.

February: Distribution of calling card handout. Continue preparation for March direct mailing.

March: Direct-mail piece.

April: Series of four pulpit testimonies on the benefits of Sunday School.

May: Promotion of special Sunday School summer calendar.

June-July: Take a break, but don't go away.

August: Design Sunday School brochure for adults.

September: Mail out Sunday School brochure to community along with quarterly to all inactive and prospects.

If those in charge of the marketing strategy prepare a yearlong calendar, it will keep them on track and working toward each marketing activity. I have noticed that if no calendar of activities is planned, the committee will feverishly work on one or two projects, only to drift through the remaining part of the year. Planning a year's calendar will help the committee or group stay on track and use its resources wisely.

If a church is serious about marketing its Sunday School or its church, it must organize to do so. Failure to organize and to place responsible people in charge of the task will doom the church to failure. Once a church attempts a marketing strategy and fails, it is difficult to lead that church to again attempt the marketing strategy. So, do it right the first time. Let's turn our attention to the world of "marketing tools" available to the church today.

5

Marketing Tools Available Today

One of the key elements in marketing is communicating or advertising the product's benefits and values. The marketing strategy is incomplete without this element. You can have the best product in the world, package it most attractively, and know just who you want to consume your product; but if you do not communicate through advertising the benefits and values of your product, it will simply sit on the shelf. If the church does not communicate the benefits and values to the unchurched, we cannot blame the them for choosing to spend their time and energy elsewhere. We must sell them on the value of the Sunday School Bible study experience and church involvement. This part of the marketing process is called *advertising*.

Types of Advertising

There are three types of advertising used in the secular world, and these should be used in the church also.

Awareness Advertising

Awareness advertising makes the prospective consumer aware of the product and how to get it. Awareness advertising can be used to introduce the product of Sunday School

52

Bible study and the church program. This kind of advertising tells what the product is. What is Bible study? More importantly, what does a person do when he becomes involved in this activity?

Also involved in awareness advertising is the "when and where of the product." Awareness advertising tells the unchurched where the Sunday School can be found and when takes place. Remember our discussion in chapter 3 about designing a menu-driven system? Be sure they know all of their choices. Be sure they know all the different "times" they can choose to take advantage of the program. Be sure and tell them "where" they can take advantage of the program.

Check your marketing strategy. Are you communicating these basics well. Say it clearly and often, in the right places and at the right times.

Selection Advertising

Selection advertising zeros in on the benefits and the values of a particular product. Selection advertising by the church seeks to convince the unchurched to select a given church activity for their expenditure of time and resources. Remember, in the coming century time will become the most important commodity. If you expect people to give their time to attending your church's Sunday School Bible-study program, you must present through selection advertising its benefits and value.

It is important for the church to remember that selection advertising is not an attempt to compel the unchurched to choose your church over another church but to compel the unchurched to choose church over other activities. We must remember that the local church is part of the universal church. We must not see ourselves in competition with each other but in competition with other activities and programs that the world offers. It is important to remember as we do selection advertising that we are presenting the benefits and values of Bible study in "the church" with a invitation to experience it in a "particular church." Again, the emphasis should be on selection of church over other activities. There are literally hundreds of activities which people may choose on Sunday. Stores are open, sports are played, and a world of activities now beckons to the unchurched. Selection advertising is a good way to convince the unchurched that we are the best choice.

Maintenance Advertising

Maintenance advertising also presents the benefits of involvement in Sunday School. Maintenance advertising is important because it keeps a hold on customers who already know the value of a product. In the church arena, we know we often lose people as fast as we gain them. It is important that we close the back door while working in other ways to open wider the front door.

If we could look into the hearts and lives of many people in our Sunday Schools today, we would see that they are close to dropping out. Look back over your church's past year and notice how many have gone from active involvement to semiactive involvement and how many have slipped from semiactive involvement to no involvement at all. If we could see into the minds of many who are active now, we would realize that their motivation for coming is something other than the benefits they derive from this experience. Many of them come out of a sense of guilt and others out of pure habit. When they learn to live with the guilt, they will be gone. When they find a habit that is more enticing, they will be gone.

Maintenance advertising reminds the participants of the benefits and the values they are receiving from participation in the Bible study experience. We'll talk more about this in Chapter 6. For now, it will suffice to say that many who actively attend your Sunday School are finding they are better people; their families are better families; their lives are richer; they have more peace, joy, and contentment, and on and on the benefits could go.

The marketing strategy for the local church should involve all three types of advertising. This is another reason why a specific person or group must be responsible for this strategy. Someone must give attention to working at all three types of advertising. Many of the tools mentioned in this chapter will do specific types of advertising. For example, "maintenance advertising" is mainly done inside the church building. Therefore, the use of things such as bulletin boards, church newsletter, Sunday bulletin, and so forth, can be used to target those who are already actively involved in your program. Awareness advertising will use tools such as newspaper, radio, television, and billboards to make people aware of the church. Other advertising tools will be used to do "selection advertising."

The twentieth century offers the church more advertising tools than ever before. In this chapter, we are going to examine approximately two dozen different tools that can be used in the marketing strategy. We need to use as many of these tools as possible. Some of these tools are going to be expensive, while others are virtually free. Some of the tools already exist and are being used for other things. The key element in the use of all marketing tools is the element of "content." The church must learn how important it is to say the "right thing to the right people at the right time in the right way." *We must learn to talk about benefits and values rather than programs and features.* Let's begin to look at the many tools available to the church today and how they can be used to market the Bible study program.

Satisfied Customers

One of the best tools available to the church today has always been available to the church. In the New Testament we find it was the main tool used by the church to reach the unchurched. With the absence of tools such as the printing press, radio and television, direct mail, computers, the church relied mainly on word of mouth. Satisfied customers became the channel for the communication of the wonderful good news of Jesus Christ and what He could do in the lives of people. Look across your congregation; satisfied customers are everywhere. These people represent one of the most valuable resources available to the church today; there are literally millions of them. The church must learn to more effectively mobilize the satisfied customers. We must involve them in the marketing of the church and the Bible study program.

Church leadership must learn that one of their most productive activities is training and motivating people to share their faith, the good news of Jesus Christ, and the benefits and values of active involvement in Bible study and church activities. We must teach our satisfied customers not to promote programs and features, but rather the benefits and values that they receive from those programs and features. The key: *The emphasis must be on benefits!* The satisfied customer becomes involved in the sharing of what the Bible study and church involvement has done for him personally.

Brochures and Calling Cards

The Sunday School marketing strategy involves mobilizing your satisfied customers so that they become involved actively in the advertising process. Teach them to do everything from parking their cars on the side of the church where passersby will see the fullest possible parking lot, to personally sharing with neighbors, friends, and coworkers the benefits of their church experience. Part of the strategy includes making "marketing pieces" available to your satisfied customers to distribute. Many churches use brochures in their visitation programs. It would be advisable to make brochures available to every church member who would be willing to give this material to persons with whom they come in contact.

The content of these brochures should focus on *benefits* of church involvement and, in particular, Sunday School. We will discuss the content of brochures and pamphlets in another section of this chapter. Some churches are using small calling card-type brochures which can be easily distributed to all who are willing to give them out in their everyday walk. You do not have to spend a fortune on this type of marketing piece. From the simplest calling card printed on one side to the folded card printed on all sides, you will spend very little. In one church we distributed one of these cards to every active Sunday School adult and youth once a month. They were encouraged to give the card to somebody during the next week. During the worship service the following week, we asked how many had been able to share an invitation to Sunday School through the use of the card. We did that for several months and it was amazing. In a few months, more and more members were using this valuable marketing piece to extend an invitation to friends, neighbors, and coworkers.

Personal Contacts

Another way to use satisfied customers is to find ways of involving them in some phase of the visitation program of your church. Visitation by the local church can involve several different types of contacts. *Life-style contacts* are made as satisfied customers rub shoulders with individuals in their everyday lives. *Assignment contacts* are those contacts made by assignment through the Sunday School. Prospects are assigned to satisfied customers who are then responsible to make a contact of some type and extend an invitation to Sunday School activities. *Door-to-door visitation* is still a viable option for the local church. Simply take a particular area of your community and knock on every door looking for prospects and sharing an invitation. Some say that door-to-door visitation is ineffective. Some pastors and churches have totally given up on any type of door-to-door strategy. I believe a church would do well to consider carefully the tremendous value of door-to-door visitation. I still hear pastors tell me that they are finding hundreds of prospects and reaching dozens through their door-to-door visitation program. Some areas of the country may be more difficult for door-to-door work, and each community should be carefully analyzed before giving up on this proven method of finding lost and unchurched people.

Another type of contact would be *contacts made by phone.* In some churches satisfied customers, either in their homes or at a convenient time at church, will make phone calls to church and Sunday School prospects. Those doing the phoning are trained in what to say and how to say it. In my opinion, a church that is not utilizing satisfied customers in this way is missing a good opportunity to involve persons who will not go door to door or talk with someone face to face.

Another area of contact by satisfied customers is *letter and card writing.* I have for a long time believed in and witnessed the power of the written word. Some satisfied customers who will not do door-to-door visitation or talk to a person over the telephone will write letters and cards. A church that really wants to increase the number of contacts being made

58

in its marketing strategy would do well to place satisfied customers in front of a desk with pen in hand. They should be given form letters that will "guide them in the freehand writing" of their letters. These form letters could be word by word or a brief outline so that the satisfied customers can put the thoughts in their own words.

In one situation, a lady commented that she had kept a letter written to her by a satisfied customer for more than six months. She had taken it out of her dresser and read it frequently. She finally committed to local church involvement and said that the letter would not let her rest until she had.

Satisfied customers can be used in so many ways to make contacts for the church visitation program. Try to organize your church so that you are using your satisfied customers in all of the areas above. Remember training is essential! Your satisfied customers need to be trained to present the benefits and values of not only the Christian life but of active participation in a Bible study program. Witness training is essential, but we need to add to this training. Teach satisfied customers how to encourage people to become a part of the Sunday School experience. If we are going to compel them in, we must be able to explain the value and benefits.

Testimonies

Another way to use your satisfied customers is through pulpit testimonies. Now remember, you have five or six different target audiences. Each of those audiences can be broken down into different age groups and types of people. If you are going use pulpit testimonies of satisfied customers, analyze who your target audience can be. The fact that these testimonies take place during the worship service means one target audience will be *active Sunday School members.* This is maintenance advertising. These testimonies will go a long way toward reminding them why they attend Sunday

School and church. It will help reinforce their commitment to continue their involvement.

A second target audience for pulpit testimonies featuring satisfied customers is *non-Sunday School church members*. These individuals may attend your worship service but seldom attend the Sunday School. Is it important that they attend Sunday School? Remember what we have said in a previous chapter. Members of your church who attend Sunday School, as well as worship services, will be more committed, more giving, more prayerful, and more involved in the total ministry of your church. Therefore, testimonies from the pulpit will be helpful as they target this second audience.

Third, pulpit testimonies can target individuals who are *inactive members of your Sunday School.* It seems to be true that as people begin to exit the church, they exit the Sunday School experience first and the worship experience last. It may be that satisfied-customer testimonies from the pulpit will reach some who are gradually drifting out of your church just before they go out the door. It may be that someone who has dropped out of Sunday School is hanging on by a thread in worship attendance. These people can be encouraged back into the Sunday School and a deeper commitment by the personal testimony of a satisfied customer.

Finally, these pulpit testimonies can be effective with those who are visiting your church and considering active involvement in the church and in Sunday School. These testimonies will encourage them by presenting the benefits of active participation in the Sunday School. Remember, one of the most powerful advertising tools available is the testimony of a satisfied customer. You might even go so far as to pick particular individuals to give testimonies at times when you know particular prospects are going to be present. For example, let's say you have a family who has told you they will be visiting your church this coming Sunday. The husband works at a large plant near your church. The wife is a homemaker. Why not arrange on that particular Sunday morning a satisfied-customer testimony by one who works at the same plant? Or by one of your homemakers who can mention the fact that her husband works at the plant? No direct comments would be made that would indicate the careful planning of this testimony, but the testimony would apply to at least one particular prospect that you expect to be in your congregation at that time. The chances of a response will be far greater as you plan carefully the use of pulpit testimonies by your satisfied customers.

In other parts of this chapter we will talk about several other ways of using your satisfied customers. Let's mention them briefly here. *Church brochures* can include testimonies of satisfied customers. If your church, as we will be suggesting, has different brochures and pamphlets for different age groups, it would be wise to use satisfied customer testimonies in those pamphlets.

Direct mail can effectively use satisfied customers, also. Testimonies can be included in the direct-mail content.

Newspaper ads, as well as *radio, television,* and even *billboards,* could include the use of satisfied customer testimonies. Don't forget the possibility of using your *Sunday bulletin,* your weekly *church mail out,* and even your *bulletin boards* inside your church to share satisfied customer testimonies. Remember, those tools using these testimonies inside the walls of the church target those who will be in those halls. Some churches have put satisfied customers testimonies on *door hangers* in areas where these are allowed.

Direct Mail

Direct mail is one of the best tools available to the church today. Direct mail is a very effective tool, if used on a regular basis and if content is well designed. Some say that direct mail does not produce results. Looking at the content and the quality of the direct-mail piece one can easily see why particular direct-mail efforts do not succeed. The quality and the content of your direct-mail piece is extremely important. If the quality and the content meet high standards, you can expect from 1 to 2 percent return. This means a mailing of 100 pieces in your community could produce one or two responses. If you mail 1,000 you can expect 20 and if you mail 10,000, you might expect from 100 to 200 responses of some type. I believe direct-mail results are cumulative. Therefore, if a church uses two, three, or four direct-mail campaigns each year, the results of each campaign will be better that the previous campaign. The results seem to snowball as people are reminded more often that the church sincerely cares about their needs.

It is important when using direct mail that the church is not offensive and that it does not seek to place the prospective consumer on a guilt trip. We have explained already why these strategies do not work. The direct-mail piece will be received with interest by a majority of the public if it is designed well. Some people think that junk mail is resented by the majority of the public. That's not really true. Many people enjoy looking through their mail every day. For some people, going to the mailbox is the most enjoyable experience of their day. If the direct-mail piece is designed in such a way as to say we are here for you and that we care about you, it will be well received by the great majority of people.

Objectives of Direct Mail

Let's think about the objectives of using direct mail. The number-one objective is to share the benefits of active involvement in the Sunday School experience. Good content must include the "benefits" and "values" derived by active involvement in the church experience. A second objective of your direct-mail campaign would be to make the church more visible. In many cases, the only people that know a church exists are those who drive by its front door. There are thousands of people around your church that do not know your church exists; but what is worse, they do not know what happens inside your church. Direct mail is one effective way of reminding them that your church exists and that a positive experience awaits them there.

A third objective of direct mail is locating prospects. Your direct mail can offer a response mechanism; a number to call if they are interested in more information, an offer of free counseling or child care. By offering these ways of responding, churches can find people who are not actively involved in another church.

A fourth objective of using direct mail can be the enhancing of the image of your church. If your church has pure motives and is really there to serve people, then tell this to the people in your community. The mere telling of this motive will help people change the way they think about your church. Over a period of several years, receiving direct mail that says we care about you, or we're here for you, or let us do something for you; the public begins to see the church in a different light.

Another objective of using direct mail is to increase contacts. We know if a church makes more contacts in the community and multiple contacts with each prospect, more response can be expected. Direct mail is one effective way to multiply the number of contacts taking place in your church area. Every time a prospect receives a piece of direct mail from your church, it is considered a contact. Can you imagine the value of making 10,000 contacts in one week? That can be done through direct mail.

A sixth objective of using direct mail is to surface needs

and even create needs in the lives of those who are in your community. The church can use direct mail to stimulate needs. As the church uses direct mail to talk about the things it can do for people, it is either surfacing needs already existing, magnifying needs that have been ignored, or creating needs that have not existed before. For instance, a person who may not feel lonely now might realize that he is indeed "friendless" when he reads a piece of direct mail which speaks about the friendship that can be found in the local church. I contend that it is very possible for a direct-mail piece to create needs within the lives of people if its content is designed with this purpose in mind. Some of the ads we have been working on in the area where I serve have as their objective the "birthing of needs."

Another objective of direct mail is to inform. It is surprising how many people I talk to who don't really know what goes on inside the church. Many people have never attended church, and many others attended a long time ago. For many of these people, the church is that "unknown" they fear. We all feel a little bit uncomfortable in unfamiliar surroundings, right! Can you imagine what it must feel like to enter the church for the first time? Some people have erroneous ideas about what happens in the church.

I remember one lady telling me that I might as well give up in my efforts to bring her into the church. She told me that she was afraid of snakes. Shocked as I was, I inquired as to what she meant by snakes. She went on to explain to me that she had always thought that's what churches like mine did; they handled snakes. She went on to explain that she didn't like snakes at all. The tragedy of this experience is not that this dear lady thought that my church handled snakes, but that my church had never taken the time to explain to this lady, or anyone else, what we did in our worship services. Take a look at all your pamphlets and bulletins, and even

MARKETING YOUR SUNDAY SCHOOL

your visitation strategy. *See if you find where you tell people what is going to happen to them when they come to church.*

One man told me that he didn't want to go back to church because he had been once before. When I asked him to explain, he went on to share that he had been put in the basement of the building where there was a room full of men from around the community. While he was trying to fill out the huge form that had been handed to him, he heard the teacher say that each of the men would have the opportunity to read out of a book of the Bible. He had never heard of that particular book. He told me that he almost had a heart attack as they worked their way around the room toward him. When they got to him, he explained to the man next to him that he didn't have a Bible. The man next to him handed him his Bible but shut it in the process. The man went on to explain that it seemed to take him an eternity to find the book of the Bible that the class had been reading from, and only after being helped by the man next to him, did he realize that he had to admit to the entire class that he had never learned how to read. He went on to say that he would probably never go back to church.

Many people have had experiences like this, and the church would do well to explain to people who either do not understand what we do or who have had bad experiences in the past, what kind of experience they will have in the church today.

Finally, one of the most important objectives of your direct mail is to share the good news of Jesus Christ. In a tactful way we need to tell people how much God cares about them. We should welcome the opportunity to share with people through direct mail that Jesus Christ is a wonderful Savior who wants to give them life abundant. We might do well to explain the wonderful aspects of heaven and the wonderful experiences that can be had in a relationship with

God. Let's talk about the peace, joy, hope, and the thrill of knowing the only God who really exists.

Producing a Direct-Mail Piece

Let's think about the steps in doing a direct-mail piece. First of all, decide who your target audience will be. If you choose to target the entire population around your church, that's all right, but future direct mail pieces might target a more specific audience. You might target those who are inactive Christians, or you might target those who went to church in their childhood but don't presently attend. You might choose to target singles or even teenagers. You might send out a piece to the senior citizens of your community. It doesn't hurt for everyone to get a piece of direct mail that is targeting someone else. You may be able to mail just to specific target audiences. There are companies in many cities that can give you the addresses of particular target audiences. You can mail to all in a particular zip code or you can mail to all the singles in a zip code. In small churches or in rural areas it would be possible to target specific people. This could be done with a little effort. Have your church family make a list of the unchurched in the community. This becomes the list for future mailings. The community could be surveyed to find where the young people live. Those young people could be targeted by particular direct-mail pieces. After you decide on your target audience, then you begin to think about who is going to mail for you. In many cities, there are companies that will provide all of the mailing help you need. Some companies will give you addresses and do the mailing for you. In other cases, the church can secure the addresses and do the mailing itself.

Designing Direct Mail

Once you've decided how you are going to mail your direct-mail piece, you need to design it. A lot of time is involved. Plan to take several months to design the direct-mail piece. One pastor commented that when he was working on a direct-mail piece it took him months to decide what he would say. He saw this as an opportunity to say something to ten thousand people in his community. He did not take that lightly. He spent time thinking through what he really wanted to say. Several drafts are important. You will see things on the fourth or fifth draft of your direct-mail piece that you did not see before. Plan to begin the design of your direct-mail piece far in advance of your target date for mailing.

Now let's talk about the importance of designing your direct-mail piece in such a way that it will be well received. First, don't let it look religious. So many brochures and pieces of direct mail have pictures of a church or a cross or even Jesus on the front. It's not that I don't like the church, the cross, or even a picture of Jesus. Direct mail that would get *my* attention would have that on the front. But I'm not the one you are trying to reach. The people that need reaching the most, the people who need to read your direct mail most are the people that are not *yet* interested in the church, in the cross, or in Jesus. So your art work, especially on the front, should not come across as religious. Other kinds of artwork are available that will get attention and draw people into the contents of your direct-mail piece. Further into the direct-mail piece, it is all right to let them know it is from your church, let them know it's about the cross, let them know it has to do with Jesus, but not too soon.

Consider the *content* of your direct-mail piece. Remember it should be full of benefits and values. *Talk about what your*

MARKETING TOOLS AVAILABLE TODAY

church is going to do for them. Talk about what a relationship with God is going to do for them. These benefits and values can be well defined and explained. Also, remember to include the location of your church. How strange it would be to see an ad for something of great benefit that didn't tell you where to get that particular product. Don't forget to put the location of your church and include a map to help those who have a more difficult time following directions. It's also important that you put the times of your services in the direct-mail piece.

Let me caution you at this point. Do not list all of the things that your church does. A list of forty-six opportunities of the week will scare an unchurched person. Notice in many pieces that we distribute to the unchurched, that too often we tell a person—who hasn't given us the first hour— about the great number of programs (hours) we promote. We might be wiser to advertise only the Sunday-morning aspect of our church experience. If a person is not able to attend on Sunday morning, then maybe we should explain that there is another opportunity for him or her to become involved. But *never* should we imply to unchurched people that there are dozens of hours when they will be expected at the church.

While knocking on a door in my own community, I looked at a visitation piece given to me by the church I was helping with visitation. I noticed that one panel listed the opportunities of the week. There were six hours of activities on Sunday, one on Monday night, one on Tuesday night, four to five on Wednesday night, one on Thursday night, and thank goodness there was nothing on the weekend until Sunday. I resisted giving out that brochure because I was afraid it would scare unchurched people away.

Another important element is the response section. You may want to include some way a prospect can respond to the benefits and values presented in the direct-mail piece. Of course, the best response is to show up at your Sunday School hour this coming Lord's Day. Active involvement in your church is surely the response you desire the most. So tell them that. Explain to them that you would like them to experience these benefits for themselves. Tell them when and where to come and offer them a phone number to call for additional information about child care and other such items. Make it easy for them to come to your church. Tell them what door to enter, tell them where child care is located, and tell them what will be expected of them while they are there.

Other response mechanisms might include a phone number to call to request a free tape or additional free literature about the church's programs. The telephone number might be given so that they could call for free counseling if they sense a need for that. Some churches now include a phone number to call if someone just needs to talk. What a powerful message that sends to the unchurched: we are here for you; call us if you need to talk. Do you see how this affects how the community views the church? Another response mechanism might be a return-mail piece, a section of your direct-mail piece that can be filled out and mailed back requesting information or a free gift. Some churches have given away a free cassette tape; others have given away free Bibles. The possibilities are endless. Put your thinking cap on!

Next comes the printing. Different types and colors of paper are available, and there is a wide range of ink colors. Many churches print their own direct-mail pieces, while others get a more professional look by having a local printer do the work. It is easy to find out how much a direct-mail piece will cost by inquiring at a neighborhood printer.

Prayer should permeate the entire process. Committees

and leaders will be wise to bathe every meeting, decision, and action with earnest, heartfelt prayer. I remember gathering with my staff and secretaries and the committee responsible as we prayed over a huge mail sack ready for mailing. We prayed that God would anoint what we were sending out and that people's hearts and minds would be touched by what was said in that direct-mail piece. We must understand that nothing we do can be effective without the anointing of the Holy Spirit of God. It is God that convicts hearts, it is God that speaks to the mind, it is God who brings the increase. But He does it through our activity!

Remember, direct mail is a good bargain. The cost of a direct-mail piece will include the printing of the piece itself, the postage used to mail it, and the cost of any addresses that you have to buy. In 1990 there were companies that would sell names in your community for $37 per 1,000. This means that you could mail to a particular person at a particular address rather than using the word *occupant* or *resident*. The cost of direct mail is not great when you consider the number of persons touched by it. Consider leading your church to budget for one or two direct-mail pieces this coming church year.

Newspapers

Newspaper ads are also a good bargain for the church that wants an aggressive marketing strategy. Newspaper ads touch a large percentage of the adult population in a given community. In the community in which I live, the daily paper touches a majority of the adult population of this area. It is important to remember several key factors when using the newspaper.

Placement is critical. Many churches put ads on religious pages in the newspaper. When I mention about advertising through the newspaper, many churches brag on how often they have an ad in the church page. Who reads the church page? Church people, of course. Churches that use the church page often do it because it doesn't cost anything. How wrong we are. It costs the time and the effort to place the ad. This time and effort is valuable when you realize that seldom is any other type of church ad used. Placement in the church page often keeps the church from using church ads in areas of the paper where they would be more effective. In my opinion, ads on the church page are have minimum impact. They may enhance the image of the church in the minds of other church people, and may stroke the ego of the church itself, but they do little to impact the unchurched.

Another important aspect of placement is putting the ad where it will target a specific audience. For instance, if you are trying to target single adults or young married couples, place your ad on the movie page. If your target audience is young homemakers, go for the grocery ad pages. If your target audience includes young men between the ages of twenty and forty, go to the sports section. Choose the section of the paper based on the target audience you're seeking to influence.

Another important facet of newspaper ads is content. Remember our key words are *benefits* and *values*. Don't simply tell the community about your church, tell your community about the benefits of attending your church. Explain to them what they will gain by attending your Bible study program. In the ads we have designed, we sought to surface the needs that people feel and the benefits that will be derived from active involvement in the Sunday School and church program. Remember, the content should not come across as religious on the surface. Churches, crosses, and other religious pictures should not be used. Church people will love it, but unchurched people will seldom give it their attention. These church images become barriers to the unchurched. Don't forget to include in your content the location of your church and a *limited* number of times they can attend. Also, consider including a response mechanism as we talked about in the previous section.

Another factor in the use of newspaper ads is *repetition.* Each of us will forget 60 percent of what we learn today within the next twelve hours. If 60 percent of what we say will be forgotten, we need to say it more often. Therefore, newspaper ads should not be used once in a while but regularly. Your ad should not be so big that you can only afford a few. Make your ads smaller so that you might use more ads with the money you have available. Be careful that you don't make your ads so small that they are not noticed and do not contain enough information. There is a happy medium here, not too large and not too small. Of course, if you have large amounts of money at your disposal, as we talked about in a previous chapter, you will do well to have the largest ads possible as often as possible.

There are ready-made ads available from many companies today. I cannot overemphasize the importance of ad content. We will talk further about that in the next chapter, but be sure and evaluate the content of ready-made ads. Do not use ads simply because they are ready-made. Many designers of ready-made ads still do not understand the importance of emphasizing benefits and values. Ads will not be effective if they do not emphasize benefits.

Newspaper ads are sold by the column inch. Normally church ads are sold at a reduced rate. In 1990, an ad in a medium-sized city was selling for approximately ten dollars per column inch, which means the ad was one column wide and one inch tall. If you want an ad that is two columns wide and three inches tall that would be considered six column inches (2 x 3). This ad would have cost approximately sixty dollars in 1990. Check with your local newspaper for the church rate as you prepare to use newspaper ads. Rates will differ from paper to paper. If you live in a area with a weekly paper, the possibilities of effective newspaper ads are increased. More people will read the weekly newspaper because it contains news about the community. Many times these newspapers are produced in areas that do not have television stations with local news. Therefore the use of newspapers in small towns is very effective.

Advertising in daily newspapers in larger cities will normally cost more. In larger daily newspapers you will want to choose the section and even the page on which you place your ad. Remember to consider the target audience and pick the section of the paper that will be read by that particular audience. Certain days are better than other days to run your ad. Think about it! The largest papers put you in competition with hundreds of other ads and articles. The smallest editions give your ads more attention but oftentimes have less circulation. Therefore, pray about your decision and consider using the paper that you think would be most effective in reaching your target audience. If you have enough budget to have a series of ads, then you can use several different days in order to touch a larger portion of the population.

All in all, newspaper ads are, in my opinion, extremely effective. They are good bargain and you can target your audience fairly well by the use of different sections of the paper. Remember, content is a primary concern and repetition is essential to effective use of the newspaper.

Radio

Radio is another good channel for your advertising. Radio has been around for many years as an advertising tool but some people believe television is a better choice. We will discuss several pros and cons about radio and television. Let it suffice here to say that radio is an effective tool. Radio is far less expensive than television; therefore, churches on a limited budget will be able to expand their advertising into radio while they cannot into television. Television ads tend to be more effective yet much more expensive. Radio can be used more often because of its lower cost, and this is valuable because of the importance of repetition. In most areas there are several radio stations, each targeting a specific type of audience. For example, you might choose to target young people by using the radio station they listen to most often. You might consider targeting the older age groups in your community through the use of country music or the easy-listening station. Baby boomers in your community could be targeted by using the easy-listening station or a station which plays tunes from the sixties and seventies.

Don't use *Christian radio stations* unless your target audience can be found there. If your target is the unchurched in your community, remember that the unchurched do not normally listen to religious radio broadcasts. Those who buy and use Christian radio hope that the unchurched would be touched by their programming. Advertisement salespersons will tell you that their audience includes the unchurched. But, survey after survey shows us that an extremely small percentage of the listening audiences of Christian radio stations is unchurched. The use of religious radio might be considered if your objective is to create a positive image for your church in the church community. It could be used as a tool for ministry to your "homebound" members. Christian radio could be considered if your target audience is your own active church members or the active church members of other churches. Your objective, of course, would be to minister to these people, but not to draw another church's members into the life of your church.

There may be some possibility that inactive Christians listen to religious radio. When a public-relations committee I worked with recently suggested the use of our funds to sponsor a gospel program, I ask them to design the ads in such a way as to speak to inactive Christians. If the money was to be spent in religious radio, I felt we should make the best use of our spots. Our stated objective was to reach the "unchurched" through our advertising dollars. (What is *your* stated purpose?) We designed our spots to target the inactive Christians who had a taste for religious music but had lost their commitment to the church.

Public-service announcements are offered by many stations but, contrary to what some people think, this is not required by law. Most public-service announcements require that you talk about a specific event. Normally these events attract churched people, not the unchurched. If your church is sponsoring events that would draw the unchurched, then the use of public-service announcements would be beneficial. Remember to include benefits in your sales pitch. Use of public-service announcements to announce revival or other regular services of your church in my opinion will not be beneficial. The use of other radio stations to promote revival, homecomings, or the regular services will also be of little benefit if your objective is to reach the unchurched. On the contrary, the use of these type announcements, along with the use of Christian radio, will sometimes lull your church into thinking that it has a good marketing strategy, when, indeed, it does not. Your church must break out of the religious market if it is serious about marketing the Sunday School and the church to the unchurched. Remember, go where the unchurched are and use your time to tell them what Sunday School can do for them, not what you want them to do for you.

There are ready-made radio ads available. Several companies are now producing ads, and you can find the companies in religious magazines or through your denominational public-relations office. Some denominational agencies are also preparing ads for use of churches and will help churches produce their own ads. Again, I would caution those in charge of the marketing strategy not to use ready-made ads out of convenience. Many of these ads do not speak to the benefits and values of the Sunday School and church and, in some cases, project the wrong message and image. *Think about your objective and use ads that will be effective.*

The cost of radio is in the medium range. It would be more expensive than using satisfied customers and newspaper ads. In 1991 a church could purchase 100 spots for approximately $950 on a local station. That same church could get 75 spots for $600 or 100 spots for $400 on a religious station. This averages out to about $10 per spot on a secular radio station and about $4 per spot on the Christian station. Again, don't be fooled into buying the cheaper Christian stations spots. Remember your target audience.

In conclusion, radio is a good buy for the money. As a church increases the amount of its budget allocated to the marketing strategy, it would do well to move from the use of direct mail and newspapers to the inclusion of radio advertising. Remember, a good marketing strategy involves more than one tool.

Television

There is a debate about the effectiveness of television in Christian circles. Some believe that televising their worship services does tremendous good while others think it does not. Some believe television advertising is effective for the church; others believe it is not. Let's give some thought to the use of television as one of the marketing tools your

church can use to present the benefits and values of attendance in your Sunday School. Television is one of the more
expensive ways to share your marketing message. Billboards
might be more expensive, but we will talk about those in
upcoming pages.

It is fairly easy to get television time for worship services
in most television markets. There is some value to televising
your worship services, but we must remember that very few
unchurched people watch religious television programs. A
small percentage of the unchurched might tune in from time
to time, but the effectiveness of televised church services is
doubtful if your target audience is the unchurched. The
main use of televising your worship service would be to
share the service with church members who are homebound
(there is great value in this) and to create a positive image
within the church community itself. Again, this does not
reach the unchurched.

Some *public-service announcements* (PSA) can be secured on
television stations, especially local stations. Again, most of
the time they ask you to announce a specific event or program. If these announcements are to be used, use them wisely to promote programs and events of particular value to the
unchurched. It would be well for the church to design programs that would meet specific needs in the lives of the unchurched. Seminars, conferences, and special services that
would meet the needs of particular audiences should be the
content of your PSA time. If your church decides to use television to present your marketing message, it will be effective
if you give "content" and "target audience" a great deal of
thought. Again, it will cost more but if rightly used, television can be a powerful marketing tool. Remember how important it is that the content center around the benefits and
values of attending Sunday School. It is important also to

create a positive image for the church, assuring that your desire to serve people comes through loud and clear. Offering free counseling or someone to talk to is a powerful way of saying, We are here for you.

Again, consider the target audiences that you are seeking to reach. This might determine what time of day you run your spots and how you design them.

There are ready-made spots available from several companies, and I believe the number of companies providing these ads to churches will increase in the future. You may design your own spots and have a local television station produce them for a fee. Some churches are able to acquire their own television equipment and tape their own spots. It is important that your ads be professionally done, if at all possible. Some denominations offer help in production. Call your denominational headquarters and ask for information.

Ad ideas are as common as everyday life. Begin to think about it and ideas will come pouring into your head. Observe how people act, what they do, and what they say. Out of these sources will come the church marketing ads for tomorrow's television.

The *cost of television* is far greater than most other tools available to the church. In 1991 a thirty-second television spot cost approximately sixty dollars to run once, compared to ten dollars for a radio spot. Advertising costs will vary in larger or smaller markets. Adding a certain percentage per year for inflation will give you some idea of what television time might be costing at present. If your church is seriously looking for new tools to use in your marketing strategy, you should check with local television stations to find out what their rates are. Rates will differ depending on the time of day you request your spot be aired. Remember, you do not want your spots airing at a time they will be wasted. Choose your time carefully, and remember, you get what you pay for.

One spot at a good time of day may be worth as much as three spots when nobody is watching. Your local television station can tell you those times when large numbers of people will be watching.

A church's marketing strategy should have as its ultimate objective the use of all marketing tools. This means that a church should continue to increase its marketing budget until radio and television are being used in its marketing strategy. *It is not enough to dabble in advertising.* You must saturate your market and use repetition to drive the point home. The church spends thousands of dollars on things that do not make a difference. Wise leaders in the future will lead churches to spend an ever-increasing amount on reaching lost people through a marketing strategy. If we are to "compel them in," it must be through the expenditure of larger sums of money on those we seek to reach. The church does not have the luxury of spending most of God's money on itself anymore. If the lost world is to be reached and if the tools available to the church today are to be used, the church must become unselfish with its funds. If the church does so, television will be a marketing reality.

Church Weekly Mail Out

Many churches have a weekly or monthly mail out that is sent to all church members and sometimes to prospects. Does your church have a weekly or monthly mail out that it uses to communicate with the church family? If your church does, there are several important questions you should ask yourself on a regular basis. Does the weekly mail out say the same thing over and over? Is the weekly mail out creating the best possible image for your church? Is the mail out a quality piece? Does someone check your mail out for typing mistakes and other errors? Do you consider who reads your weekly mail out and are you targeting specific audiences with it? Do the contents of your mail out come across as mostly positive or negative? Do you see the weekly mail out as just another task for the week or one of your best opportunities to communicate with a large audience?

In many cases, I find several problems with weekly or monthly mail outs I evaluate. Most of them repeat the same thing, from mail out to mail out. We put a list of the opportunities of the week (just about everybody's memorized this list by now). I would guess that this list of opportunities is seldom read. We might do better to emphasize specific programs from time to time or even in regular rotation. Most of the time articles written by church staff are too wordy, preachy, and negative. The front of the mail out too often does not give the feeling that the church cares about its image.

As a church evaluates its mail out, it needs to realize that the weekly or monthly mail out is one of the many tools that can be used to market the Sunday School. A weekly mail out is one tool that will cost nothing. That's right, it's already available, already paid for, already waiting for your use. Let's think about which target audiences you can reach with your weekly mail out.

You can talk to your active Sunday School members about the benefits and values they receive from attending. Remember one of the most important target audiences will be those who are already attending (maintenance advertising). You don't want to lose them. Help them realize what they are getting out of the Sunday School; they may not have thought about it for a long time. Remember, attendance by their family in the Sunday School of your church may have gone a long way toward keeping their family together, keeping their children off drugs, teaching their children moral standards, creating a better relationship between husband and wife, and so much more. It maybe that they do not even realize the tremendous benefits they have been receiving by being active in Sunday School. Tell them about these benefits through your weekly mail out.

A second target audience you can reach through weekly mail outs is non-Sunday School church members. A fairly large group of people come to your worship services on Sunday but have never seen the value of the Sunday School experience. Their perception of what the Sunday School is all about and who should attend may be in error. Here is your chance to talk with them about the benefits and values of active Sunday School involvement! Remember, the way to bring this group in is to help them understand what they will get from the Sunday School experience. Convince them it will be well worth one additional hour.

Another group that you can target with your mail out is inactive Sunday School members. These are the folks that are on your Sunday School roll, but seldom if ever attend. Your weekly mail out already goes into their homes. Why not use it to "compel them back in"? Remember that you do not want to use guilt, but you want to sell them on the benefits of the Sunday School experience. If you are going to target inactive Sunday School members, you may want to plan a complete strategy including visits by the Sunday School classes and special letters over a period of several months. In my opinion, a concentrated effort to reach the inactive Sunday School members that involves the use of your bulletin, weekly mail out, Sunday School class visitation, staff visitation, letters, and phone calls will reach one out of every three inactives that still live within the ministry range of your church.

The final group that you might target with your mail out is inactive church members. I might even include the unchurched. At first I did not feel that the mail out could touch these two target audiences. I have changed my opinion, based on a recent visit in a neighborhood home. The man I visited with was not a Christian and his wife was an inactive church member. He mentioned in passing that he had read about the church most recently in the mail out that comes into their home weekly. I was surprised to hear that an unchurched person was reading the weekly mail out from his wife's church (remember she is an inactive member). When I asked him if he read the mail out on a regular basis he responded, "I look at it very often." If he is representative of even a small number of unchurched and inactive members, it may be that there is some value to marketing the Sunday School in your mail out with these two groups in mind.

If you are going to target the unchurched and inactive church members, you might consider several possibilities. On a regular basis market the Sunday School with these two target groups in mind. They just might read it! When you are targeting these groups, make sure that you are sending to all of your prospects on your prospect roll. You may even decide to do a mass mailing to all of the homes in your community with those particular mail outs. This particular mail out can be given to members on Sunday to give to unchurched and inactive church members while they are at work or school.

Remember, your mail out is "free." By that I mean it has already been paid for and is already being used. What you must do is find the wasted space and reallocate that to marketing of your Sunday School. Rather than looking for filler each week, someone must give consideration to marketing the Sunday School in that space. The Sunday School director or the marketing director, the pastor or one of the other staff should use that space to talk about the benefits of active Sunday School attendance. It may be that the Sunday School director or marketing director needs to request space in the mail out for this purpose on a regular basis.

Finally, let's think about the contents. If you choose to use your mail out to market the Sunday School, the key word as always is *benefits*. Write articles about the benefits of the Sunday School experience. You may want to involve certain satisfied customers in this process. These faces and names will often be recognized by those who read the mail out. They will be interested in what these individuals say about their Sunday School experience (and hopefully, influenced by them). Use the mail out to promote attendance at special Sunday School events, especially high-attendance days. Traditionally, we have done this, but if it is not coupled with "benefits," we may be speaking into the wind. Most people are not motivated by our desire to have big numbers in attendance. At least those that are not that interested in the Sunday School or the church in the first place. At times our high-attendance days, our round-up days, our "beat the high attendance of last year campaigns" cause people to think that all we care about is numbers. In your next promotion of high-attendance day or some special Sunday School attendance drive, talk about what it will mean to those who will come on that day. Take time to look at the lesson for that day. Tell them what they are going to experience and explain to them the benefits of paying the price on that day to attend.

If there are special lessons of interest to any one of your target groups, use the mail out to them about it. In all of my reading of church mail outs, I have yet to find one that ever mentioned the lesson for the upcoming Sunday. The lessons may have fantastic benefits for everyone who attended, but those benefits are never mentioned before the actual hour of the class. Take time to look at the Sunday School lessons coming up for the next quarter. Is there one of exceptional value to the unchurched? If so, tell them about it!

Stay positive in your content. If you constantly fuss at the people for not coming, you are using negative motivation. Why not try a new direction? Rather than telling them how bad they are for not coming, begin to tell them the tremendous blessings they would receive if they did come. Get specific! Let them know exactly what they are going to get out of it. Talk about a different blessing and benefit each time. I think if we knew the truth, we would find that many have quit reading the mail out or at least certain paragraphs because they know they are going to get a lecture. Remember, guilt does not work on most people today. What does work is, "What will it do for me?"

Your mail out can be used as an effective tool to reach all of your target audiences; especially your inactive church members and your non-Sunday School church members. It is also effective in maintenance advertising directed toward your active Sunday School members. If you do not presently have a church mail out, you will want to consider budgeting for a "monthly" mail out in the upcoming year. As soon as possible move to a weekly mail out. If rightly used it can be a powerful tool in your communications toolbox.

Sunday Bulletin

Most churches have a Sunday bulletin that is given out every Sunday to those who attend the worship service. It usually includes the order of worship for both Sunday morning and Sunday night and a list of the activities of the upcoming week along with a prayer list and other announcements about church activities. If your church already prints a Sunday bulletin, why not use it to market the Sunday School?

There are several target audiences you can communicate with through the Sunday bulletin. Unlike the weekly mail out, this will not be read by many unchurched or inactive Christians. They are not present on Sunday to receive the bulletin. It is possible that "prospects" who are attending can be affected by the content of this bulletin. It is also possible that inactive Christians who drift back in from time to time can be affected by this bulletin. The use of the bulletin to market the Sunday School would be well timed if used on high-attendance day, a special revival, or some other church event that draws additional people into the worship service.

Whenever your church is having a special event such as a revival, concert, drama, or some other event, a bulletin would be in order. Remember, you may be able to communicate with people through this bulletin at a special event that you would not be able to communicate with at other times. Therefore, for Vacation Bible School Family Night you should have a special bulletin with content targeting those who will come just for that event. If you are having a revival, a different bulletin every night would be appropriate. The content should be designed to convince people of the value of the Bible study experience. The same is true of any other event held in your church.

As you consider the Sunday bulletin someone needs to request space to be used for the marketing of the Sunday School. This can be a regular section used every Sunday or, better still, a special series about once a quarter. If space is not available on the pages of the Sunday bulletin, request that you be allowed to insert a special page from time to time that markets the Sunday School. If secretarial time is not available, offer to type and insert it yourself. There are plenty of satisfied customers in your Sunday School who would gladly give the time to prepare a special promotional piece about attending Sunday School.

Let's think for a minute about the target audiences you could communicate with through the Sunday bulletin. First, there are active Sunday School attenders, those who regularly attend your Sunday School and worship experiences.

Most of them would get the Sunday bulletin. I say most of them, even though I've been to many churches where the bulletins are simply laid on a table for those who, "know where to find them." I have noticed that when someone from the platform says, "Look in your bulletin," many heads turn to look for a bulletin only to realize they "did not have enough sense" to pick one up. If your Sunday's bulletin is important and worth the time you put into it, then it surely must be worth the energy of two persons at each door, giving one to everyone who walks through. It will cost you a little more money to print an additional dozen or so, but wouldn't it be well worth it? If your bulletin is not important then why not just quit printing it ? Isn't it ironic that we expect people who seldom attend or who have come for the first time to have some sixth sense telling them that they are supposed to walk over to a table and pick up the Sunday bulletin?

Active Sunday School attenders need to be encouraged to continue attending. Remember what we said in an earlier chapter: Some of them are one day away from dropping out. Market the Sunday School benefits to those who are regularly attending so that you can keep them coming. You might say you want to "compel them to keep coming in."

A second group you can target with your Sunday bulletin is non-Sunday School church members. This hits the nail right on the head. These folks are already in the church, they are already dressed, and they are waiting for you to convince them to come an hour earlier to attend the Sunday School experience. Remember in a previous chapter why we want them to come to Sunday School. Would it benefit, not only them, but also the church? So take the time to use that Sunday bulletin to talk to them about attending Sunday School.

Tell them about the benefits. Put satisfied-customer testimonies in that bulletin from time to time. Use this in conjunction with other strategies directed toward this target group.

A third group that we could target with the Sunday bulletin is inactive Sunday School members. As active members of a church become inactive, they exit through the worship service. By that I mean they quit attending Sunday School first. Because of some degree of loyalty or guilt, they continue to attend the worship service for a time. Notice that you'll see them there but not in Sunday School. You may encourage them back into the Sunday School but to no avail. The truth is they are simply on their way out, and they stop by the worship service a few times. It may take weeks or months before they make the final break into the ranks of the inactive.

This is your chance to draw them back into deeper involvement in the church. Through the use of your Sunday bulletin you can speak to those in your congregation this Sunday who are on their way out. Remind them of the benefits they will be giving up. Remind them of the benefits they were experiencing while they were actively involved in Sunday School. If you don't use your church bulletin and other marketing strategies to catch these people before they leave the worship door the last time, you have deprived them of the benefits of the Sunday School experience and of the church itself. You also deprive your church of an active member. Don't let them go!

There are other groups you can touch with your Sunday bulletin if you use it in some special ways. Print enough of your Sunday bulletins to make several available to those satisfied customers who really would like to give one away at work or across the fence to the neighbor who doesn't attend church. Make sure they know these are available and that you don't want to throw them in the trash. You may want to print the extra copies during a special series that emphasize the Sunday School and its benefits. Explain to your members what you have in mind. Your members should understand that on a regular basis they can take their Sunday bulletin and give it away to someone. Remember, this will not be of much advantage to you if your Sunday bulletin does not have content that would draw people into your worship service and Sunday School. Quit wasting space and start saying something of substance in that Sunday bulletin.

That brings me to the content of your Sunday bulletin. It would be much like the content of your weekly mail out in the areas you are using to market the Sunday School. Remember the key word again is *benefits*! Do not use guilt! It does not work. Emphasize special studies. Don't forget to offer special interest classes and to give them plenty of notice as to when those classes will be meeting. Again, use testimonies of satisfied customers and always project a positive image. For example, it might not be the wisest to always list enrollment and attendance. What that says to a lot of people is that a whole bunch of people who are enrolled don't ever attend, and many of those who attend this Sunday won't be back next Sunday. Ask yourself, Why do we list the enrollment in particular places? It's important to list it in some places, but not so important in others. Let's not be shackled by tradition but be wise. Use your Sunday bulletin's content to correct misunderstandings. For instance, is Sunday School just for kids? If it's not, tell them so in the Sunday bulletin. Don't forget to use it to publicize any special series of lessons that would have special appeal. Tell them about upcoming lessons and remember to always emphasize the benefits.

Keep in mind that calendar of marketing activities I talked about in a previous chapter. I don't believe you will do much

88

of what we are talking about now unless somewhere on that calendar you have designated a particular month to give emphasis to marketing the Sunday School in your bulletin. The entire year should be full of several different strategies to market your Sunday School. Use that calendar of marketing activities.

Port-of-Entry Classes

Let's talk for a few minutes about some special Sunday School classes that are what I call "port-of-entry" classes. By port of entry, I mean that these classes become entrance points for people who are coming into the church. These classes are of special interest and may be Bible centered or simply Bible based. People become interested in the subject matter and through that are drawn into the Sunday School program of the church.

There are several objectives to organizing this type of Sunday School class. These classes can minister to specific areas of need. Some of the classes touch people at the point of their hurt and address specific crises in their lives.

A second objective is to make the church more relevant to the unchurched. Often we find the unchurched public feels that what is taught in the Sunday School is not relevant to their lives today. This comment is more often heard today than ever before. We seldom address those issues that impact the lives of people in their everyday walk. When we do, it seems that we barely touch the issue then move on to another subject. Some port-of-entry classes can address those relevant issues and help the unchurched realize that the church does not have more to say to their everyday life.

Another objective is to bring the unchurched into contact with the church itself. Port-of-entry classes are the first contact some of the unchurched will have with the experience of Bible study or with the church itself. It may be the first time that some of them have had contact with the church after many years of absence.

A final objective of the port-of-entry classes is to enroll and involve the unchurched in the ongoing Sunday School program of the church. This is done by using the port-of-entry classes to express concern for the unchurched, touch them at the point of their need, and invite them to be a part of the ongoing program.

Several weeks before the end of a port-of-entry class, tactfully emphasize that the ongoing Bible-study program of the church addresses needs also. Teachers of the port-of-entry classes should carefully plan their strategy at this point. For several weeks before the end of the special class, those attending should be given an opportunity to enroll in the ongoing Sunday School program of the church. Those regular members of the Sunday School who have chosen to be involved in the port-of-entry class can at this time give their personal testimony as to what the ongoing Bible-study program means to them.

The time and place of port-of-entry classes are important. These classes can be offered on Sunday or on some other day of the week. I have seen it work both ways. Classes can also be offered in the church setting or in some neutral site in the community around the church. I have seen classes of this type meeting in community centers, fire stations, apartment complexes, and other such areas outside the actual church building. I have also seen port-of-entry classes work effectively inside the church building. Classes can meet at the same time the regular Sunday School is meeting or at some other time during the week. I remember one class that met on Wednesday morning at 8:30, targeting those mothers who brought their children to the kindergarten. I remember another class that met on a Thursday morning in a community center. I remember a third class that met in the church building on Sunday morning at 9:45 with great success.

Let's talk about the makeup of these classes. They can address such needs as building a better marriage, getting a good start as newlyweds, dealing with grief, or caring and feeding for a first child.

We tried a class directed toward those who were about to be married or had just been married. This class was well received even though it was held in the church at the regular Sunday School hour. We targeted those individuals who we knew were about to be married or who had just recently been married. The strategy involved choosing a couple to teach this class that could effectively communicate to young newlyweds. The content was chosen carefully and designed to include all of the areas of concern to newlyweds. We targeted our audience by watching the local newspaper carefully and pulling from it the names of those people who were about to be married or who had been married recently. We found that we could get the address of the couple (in most cases, the bride) by calling the bride's parents, who were listed in the newspaper announcement. We found that the parents of the bride were extremely positive about involving their daughter and new son-in-law in anything that would help the marriage succeed. Most of the time they gave us an address where we could send a personal invitation to both the bride and the groom. Letters were designed for this purpose. The letter explained several important details such as content and the length of the class and that there was no obligation of any kind. The letter also explained all the different areas of married life that would be addressed. They included everything from "how to work your finances" to "sexual adjustment" to "how to communicate well" to "how to end an argument." This class received an overwhelming response, and the church had achieved several of the objectives we have pointed to earlier.

Another class that might be well received would be a class on building a better marriage. This class would be for people who have been married for awhile and want to make their marriage even better. This class deals with many of the same issues the newlywed class deals with, but the target audience is different. Publicity for this type of class is done through the media. Special guests are brought in to address the class from time to time and to help those who are attending strengthen their marriage.

Another port-of-entry class might be one that deals with grief. The loss of a loved one is a tragic experience which produces great need in the life of the remaining partner. The target audience for this type of class can easily be surfaced by again reading the local newspaper and carefully listing all of those who lose loved ones. There is good material available for this type of class and tactful letters sent to those who have lost loved ones can produce good results. The media can also be used in publicizing this type of class and, most importantly, your own members can invite people they know who have lost a loved one.

Another class that might receive good response is a class for new parents. Birthing their first child is often a little scary for young married couples. This class could involve local doctors and paramedics in teaching new parents how to handle their newborn. The study can include everything from decorating a child's room to how to keep the child from choking. During all of these classes, remember to emphasize the biblical perspective. Names of people who might be interested in this class could be obtained through several sources: the local hospital, local pediatricians' offices, even diaper services, and so forth. There is a way and serious creativity can find it!

These alternative classes may find some resistance in the average church. As we have explained earlier, new things are not always accepted easily. It would be good to start gradually with one or two classes and move to an entire department designed specifically for alternative classes. The church should understand that these classes are not designed to compete with existing classes, but to enhance the total program of the church and to draw the unchurched into the fellowship. It is important to move slowly and take the time to sensitize your church to the need for these classes. Involve as many of your own people in the planning and implementation of this program as possible. I think that the Bible study program of any church would be enhanced by a more-menu driven approach. People should have a choice as they come into the church as to what area they will study. This will not take away from Bible study, but will, in the long run, enhance it. I hope your church will begin to look in to the possibility of alternative classes which become "ports of entry" for your Sunday School program.

Vacation Bible School

Let's turn our attention now to the Vacation Bible School, which is normally a part of the ongoing Sunday School Bible-study program. Vacation Bible School is a powerful tool for reaching unchurched people if it is used with that goal in mind. In my own experience, I have found that most churches are not using Vacation Bible School to its fullest potential to reach people. Even though this is true, thousands of children and even adults are being reached through Vacation Bible Schools each year. Think what could be done if every VBS became effective in compelling the unchurched in.

Let's look at some ways Vacation Bible School can be used

to market the Sunday School and introduce adults to Bible study.

Using the Vacation Bible School Transfer Plan, those who are enrolled in Vacation Bible School are invited to transfer that enrollment into Sunday School. I have found that many churches completely neglect this wonderful opportunity to draw individuals into the ongoing Bible study program. Teachers should be trained in the importance of this activity and should be required to invite every person attending their class to transfer into Sunday School. Your church can find ways to creatively carry out this process.

Another way is through the discovery of prospects. When I visit in churches I often ask about the prospects they discovered in the Vacation Bible School. I am often taken to the church office where we look, for what seems to be for hours, for the stack of Vacation Bible School enrollment forms. Once they are found we have to thumb through them to see which ones were not already involved in the church. First, there are not that many and, second, those we found had not been followed up for active visitation and enrollment in regular Sunday School.

Following up on those prospects discovered in Vacation Bible School is essential! Prospects must be visited by not only the Sunday School staff but by those who have been teaching them during VBS week. Sometimes schedules will allow your regular Sunday School teachers teach the same age group in Vacation Bible School. This is an extension of their regular Sunday School ministry and helps the children get to know them. This makes entrance into the ongoing class much easier.

Another way to use your Vacation Bible School is to teach the "benefits of Sunday School participation" in the Vacation Bible School itself. It would be possible to add these benefits into the agenda for your VBS teachers. A special

94

training session could be held to teach teachers how to do this. We have listed these benefits in another section of the book, but of main importance is the fact that teachers of the Vacation Bible School realize that bring new people into Sunday School is one of their main objectives for the week.

Another way to use the Vacation Bible School is to leave things undone. By that I mean to leave the lesson somewhat unfinished on purpose. Teachers could encourage pupils to come back on Sunday to finish the work. Even the idea of leaving some of the crafts unfinished to be picked up on the following Sunday might be helpful. Smooth transition can be made back in to the ongoing Sunday School. Again, this is why it would be good to use Sunday School teachers in the Vacation Bible School wherever possible. The fact that many mothers work has caused some churches to go to a nighttime Vacation Bible School which I have found has been very effective in many situations.

The final way to use the Vacation Bible School to market the Sunday School is your Vacation Bible School Family Night. Most churches have one but don't use it effectively. Too often the family night is simply a gathering where we express appreciation to those who have worked in the Vacation Bible School and parade the kids before their parents in some type of skit or presentation. We have even taken this opportunity to "preach" at those unchurched who are present. I think there is a better way to use Family Night to market the Sunday School.

First, set a new objective for the night itself. It is not to express appreciation to your workers; you can do that in a dozen other ways. It is not to preach to those whom you have an opportunity. If you do your job well that night you'll have opportunity on the Sundays to follow. It is not to parade the children in front of the parents in presentations or skits. That can be done to a lesser degree.

So, if we don't do all of these things, what do we do with Vacation Bible School Family Night? First, we let the entire church and our Vacation Bible School staff know about the objective of Family Night. It is simply to encourage the unchurched who have been involved in our Vacation Bible School either as pupils or as parents to see the value of ongoing participation in Bible study. Sunday School and church members should be encouraged to attend Family Night in order to have the "unchurched" rub shoulders with the "churched." Special greeters should be selected to be at all entrances and ushers should be in the parking lots to make sure every person who enters the church that night senses the warmth and friendliness that is a part of your church. Too often this is the night when nobody is there to greet the newcomers. The lights don't get turned on outside the building. Some of the doors don't get unlocked. The air conditioners didn't get turned on. (Does it sound like I have been in *your* church?)

A special brochure should be printed for that night. Let's think for a moment about the contents of that brochure. Don't list the names of all the teachers. Again, there are other ways to express appreciation to those who have faithfully worked in the Vacation Bible School. Also, don't list the order of your service. Those who are present are going to do whatever you tell them to do as you go through the evening. What you do want to put in that brochure is a big "thank you" to all of the children and adults who attended the Vacation Bible School and to the parents who allowed their children to be a part of the church this week.

Second, you will want to brag on the children. Which of us parents doesn't like to hear somebody tell us what a great kid we have? Tell everyone that this has been the best group that you have ever had in Vacation Bible School and one of the smartest. (I think if you observe carefully you might be able to say that.) Say in this brochure "what" you taught those who attended Vacation Bible School. These are some of the same "benefits" of attending Sunday School on a regular basis. Make sure you are able to say you taught the children the importance of obeying their parents. You also have taught the children how much the parents love them, and at what cost they provide food, housing, and clothing for their children. Tell the parents that you taught their children about the work ethic and how hard the parents work in order to make a living for the family. This helps the unchurched understand that there are benefits to having their children at the church. Don't neglect to tell them that this is what you teach on an ongoing basis in Sunday School.

Another section might offer the benefits of attending Sunday School. Oh yes, and don't forget the benefits of being involved in your church. If your church has free counseling tell them about it. If your church offers kindergarten, day care, or mother's day out, tell them about that also. You decide what are the benefits and the special services your church offers and realize this is an important place to make those benefits visible.

Make the evening casual. Consider having a carnival-type atmosphere to draw the kids back. The gathering where you make your presentation can easily take place in the fellowship hall or the sanctuary. I believe it is important to have the group come inside the church building for the actual Family Night service.

Every community is different and you might want to give a great deal of consideration to when you have your Family Night. Don't do it the way you have always done just because of that fact.

Vacation Bible School can effectively enhance the image of your Sunday School program and actually draw new individuals into the program if it is used for that purpose. Take the time this year to staff your Vacation Bible School with the best possible people and train them how to use the Vacation Bible School to reach the unchurched and market the Sunday School. It goes without saying that the pastor, church staff, and person or persons involved in marketing the Sunday School must be very involved in a Vacation Bible School program.

Bulletin Boards and Wall Space

One area that is often overlooked in marketing the Sunday School or the church is the bulletin board and wall space in the church. Wall space is everywhere and oftentimes good wall space is unused. Bulletin boards are often full of old stuff which is turning brown and most of what is on the bulletin board is maintenance oriented. Why not use some of these areas to market the Sunday School? They are free for the taking and cheap for the keeping!

Think about the target audiences you could reach by using this marketing tool. First of all, you can do maintenance marketing with your active Sunday School members. If you remember what we have said about this group already, you will remember how important it is to actively market the Sunday School to those who are already consumers. Remind them of the value and benefits that they are deriving from Sunday School involvement.

Another target audience would be non-Sunday School worship attenders. Again, the value of drawing these worship attenders into the Sunday School program of your church has great return for both the church and them personally. The wall space and the bulletin boards that are in view of those who attend your worship service (but not your Sunday School) ought to be used to market the Sunday School experience. Those areas which these worship attenders view might include the water fountain, the church foyer, and those areas where rest rooms are located. There is a lot to be said about white space but too much "white space" which is "wall space" might be "wasted space." Of course, the use of these areas will market your Sunday School to the unchurched who might visit your worship services.

You can market your Sunday School through the use of bulletin boards and wall space to the unchurched at other times also. The unchurched will frequent your church building for things such as weddings, community activities, kindergarten or day care, and funerals. I would suggest that the church attempt to have as many of these type activities as possible because they draw the unchurched into the building. Your church might consider having special bulletin boards that are used for weddings. These bulletin boards can be designed to market the Sunday School and be put up when weddings and receptions are held. If the reception is to be held in your fellowship or banquet hall, make sure these bulletin boards are placed in those areas if possible. If it is not possible to place them in that area for decoration purposes, make sure they are placed in the hallways, entrance ways, and rest room areas leading to the reception area. If I were a pastor, I would have two or three of these boards to be used in this way. I might build the content around Sunday School's benefits for marriages and families. You may host community activities in your church from time to time. Some churches are used for voting and other community meetings. If this is the case, these bulletin boards should be in the areas where the unchurched would see them. If you have a kindergarten, day care, or parents' night out, make sure that you market the Sunday School to those unchurched who are going to be frequenting your building because of these programs.

In one church I visited there were dozens of children (and their parents) coming into the building every week because of the day-care program. When we analyzed the wall space beside which these people walked, we found that we were doing nothing to encourage these people into active involvement on Sunday. After some deliberation, we decided the church should take the following actions. They would create a hospitality center at the entrance. They would enlist greeters who would be present each morning to greet those who came in. A low-key greeting involved no more than the opening of the door for folks as they came in. We made sure that the greeters would be identified as part of the friendly church family. Coffee was made available at the hospitality center for those who chose to be sociable. We also used the hallways leading to the day-care area to market the benefits of the Sunday School. Special bulletin boards were erected and the wall space was used to communicate the benefits of ongoing Sunday School involvement to the family unit. Making a better marriage and the rearing of our children were all emphasized in a tactful way.

Some churches still conduct funerals in their buildings. If this is the case, the church would do well to use its bulletin boards and wall space to market the Sunday School to those who attend the funerals. Of course, at this delicate time the contents of the board must be in good taste lest you do more harm than good.

Let's discuss the contents of these bulletin boards and wall space. First of all, the contents should be well designed and of good quality. Most churches, with some degree of effort, can put up attractive displays about the benefits of the Sunday School. Don't be guilty of putting up material on your wall space that is not attractive and could be criticized by some church members. The contents should be the benefits and the value of Sunday School involvement. Talk about what you can do for them. You can use the wall space to emphasize a special series of Bible studies or special subjects that will be upcoming. Plan far enough ahead so you have good promotion time available for the materials you prepare. You might also consider in your content testimonies of satisfied customers. Large 8 x 10 pictures of individuals who actively attend your church, along with a short testimony in large letters, can be very effective. When you request pictures for these, please ask for casual dress and life-style settings.

Let's think about the cost of using your bulletin boards and wall space. In many churches there would be no cost at all. In other churches the addition of bulletin boards in specific target areas would cost very little. The main cost might be that of attractive materials out of which to build your display. Again, don't be sloppy. Design your materials to be very attractive. You might be able to enlist (even hire) a local sign painter or artist to do a professional job on your display. This can be especially cost effective if you are planning to use the display over a period of many months. Think about your bulletin board and wall space as a newspaper ad or even a billboard. You want to get your main idea across, and you want to get the attention of the person who is walking by the display area.

The next time you are in your church take special notice of your bulletin boards and wall space. Are they being used as an effective tool to market your Sunday School and church? Are they being wasted for the most part? You might want to visit other churches in your community during the week and observe their use of bulletin boards and wall space. Some great ideas as to how to do effective bulletin boards can be gleaned from this type of visit. There are also many periodicals on how to design effective bulletin boards. Visit your local Christian book store or the local school-supply store.

Pulpit Spots

Another tool that can be effectively used in marketing your Sunday School is the pulpit. When people gather in the sanctuary for worship you have a excellent opportunity to market the Sunday School from the pulpit. Normally, the only pulpit time given to the Sunday School is the time for Sunday School announcements and report. I find that many churches are now deleting even this visibility for the Sunday School. I would suggest that time be given for the Sunday School announcements every Sunday morning. This time should be short, thirty to sixty seconds is adequate. Some things to keep in mind as the Sunday School leader makes announcements would be the following. Never be negative. If attendance is up talk about it. If attendance is not up, talk about the benefits of active involvement in Sunday School, or talk about the wonderful lesson and the most important point of the lesson for that morning. Or talk about an exciting series of lessons that will be upcoming. Don't use this time to talk about the people who weren't there and fuss at the people who were there. The Sunday School leader might use this time to praise a particular Sunday School class or teacher. Often the very demeanor with which the report is made implies things aren't going so well. This is not how the secular world advertises a product, even if the product were losing sales. You don't tell folks, "Not many people are buying our product but we sure hope you will consider it," do you? Of course not! You lift up the benefits and value. You pump the people up about what they are going to get out of it if they will consume the product.

You might be asking, "Who is my target audience at this time?" Remember the importance of maintenance marketing for those who are already actively involved in your Sunday

School. Reinforce their active involvement during these pulpit spots. Remember there are a number of people who attend worship whom you want to attend Sunday School. This is another chance to address this target audience. On many occasions you will be addressing other target groups as well.

During the Sunday School announcement time or, better still, in a special spot in the worship service, a few minutes could be given to testimonies of satisfied customers. Use these satisfied customers to target your audience. When you pick a satisfied customer to give a pulpit spot, think about who you are trying to communicate with in the congregation. If you are targeting senior adults, put senior adults in the pulpit. If you are targeting the factory worker that thinks Sunday School is just for kids, put another factory worker in the pulpit to tell why he attends Sunday School. If you are trying to convince singles who attend just the worship service to get involved in the Sunday School, then put singles in your pulpit to talk about what they get out of Sunday School.

It is not a bad idea to have the pastor use his influence to promote Sunday School attendance. A wise pastor wants everybody to attend Sunday School. The pastor can easily find times to brag on the value of a specific lesson, to talk about upcoming lessons that he believes will really help the congregation, or to talk about a special class that is being offered that meets a special need. The pastor might even have a pastor's class to which he selfishly invites those that are not attending anywhere else. If the pastor talks about the value of Sunday School attendance often enough, some people attend simply because he believes it is right. Let's don't forget there is great value to bragging on a class that is progressing or on a teacher that is doing an excellent job.

These pulpit spots could also be given by the Sunday

School director or some other staff member. Whoever does it, make sure that person understands the psychology of the pulpit spots. Again, you are not there to scold people for not coming but to tell them about the benefits and value of becoming involved in the Sunday School Bible study experience. If you don't *plan* to do this, it won't get done. Don't forget to use the marketing activity calendar to schedule times when you are going to use the pulpit to market the Sunday School.

Brochures and Pamphlets

I have noticed that churches will send people on visitation with nothing to leave with the people they visit. Almost half the time, no one is at home. Why not provide something to leave every time you find the resident not at home?

I am surprised how many churches have no brochure at all. Since we began our emphasis on marketing the church and the Sunday School in my area, dozens of our churches have designed and provided brochures to their people.

I am surprised also how many churches have out-of-date brochures. Their brochure has either been made out of date by change of pastor or because they changed the times of one or more of their regularly scheduled meetings. I am also surprised how many brochures are poorly designed. They simply don't communicate the values and benefits of the church. We tend to be program oriented, so we simply tell about our programs. Why not go one step further and explain the benefits of participation in our programs? I believe we are leaving too much to the imagination. We are naive to believe most people who are not in church understand the value of being involved in church events, even Sunday School and worship.

Brochures and pamphlets should be used in all visitation activities of the church. Even better, brochures should be given to the unchurched at every opportunity. This can be done by distributing the brochures to satisfied customers so they can give them away in the marketplace, at work, at neighborhood events, wherever they go. These brochures can also be used in direct mailings.

What about target audience? Sunday School brochures should target everyone who needs to attend Sunday School. The church might have a general Sunday School pamphlet that talks about the values and benefits of the Sunday School experience. It might explain what we do in Sunday School and even what we don't do. Many people are not sure what will happen to them if they attend the Sunday School experience. Some people have had negative experiences in the past. Remember the lady who thought our church handled snakes? Or the man who couldn't read being asked to read? It is possible that many unchurched have fears about what we do in the Sunday School itself.

Has the church taken the time to design materials to explain to people what they will do and they will not be asked to do when they attend our Sunday School? Have we explained what they will experience when they come? Is it possible that we have been naive in thinking that they already know what happens inside the walls of our church? If our objective is to compel people into the church and into Sunday School, why have we neglected to prepare material that would make them feel more comfortable when they come?

It might seem I'm going a little bit overboard to make the next suggestion. I think we ought to have a Sunday School brochure for every age group. By that I mean that there ought to be a brochure or pamphlet that specifically sells young people on the value and benefits of coming to youth

Sunday School. The pamphlet ought to "speak their language." It ought to include testimonies by other young people that enjoy the Sunday School experience. It should be designed in such a way as to easily be carried around by teenagers to give to their friends at school.

What about a pamphlet designed just for single adults? Approximately one out of every three adults is single. Why not have a pamphlet that talks about their specific needs and the way the Sunday School can benefit their lives? These can be used by other satisfied singles to invite their friends at work, in their neighborhood or apartment complex.

What about a pamphlet for senior adults? They are the fastest-growing segment of our population and will continue to grow in the coming years. Why not address the needs of senior adults in a senior-adult brochure? Distribute it where senior adults congregate and give it to your satisfied senior adult customers to give to their friends.

What about a children's pamphlet? This pamphlet could be designed to be easily carried to school and given to friends. Can you see your third graders inviting their friends at school and giving them this brochure? (I hope you can.)

It might seem like a lot of work to design all of these pamphlets, and I am being naive to think that very many churches would go to this much trouble. But I believe if our main objective is to compel people to come in, we have neglected an important area. We must communicate the benefits and values of coming to church and Sunday School in the language of every person we seek to reach. We have to address specific needs and show how the Sunday School and church can meet those needs. We are not talking about a lot of money. If they are designed well, these pamphlets can last for many years before they must be updated. It might be wise for a church to budget for a different age group brochure every year. Within three or four years a church could have all the brochures it needs to attract every age group into its Sunday School.

Let's talk for a minute about the content of pamphlets and brochures. We will deal more with content in the next chapter as we talk about content in all of the marketing tools. But let's touch on a few points here.

First, don't make it "churchy" in appearance. By that I mean, symbols such as the church, the cross, the empty tomb, and even the face of Jesus might be very attractive and appealing to you and me but a barrier to the unchurched. They are not really excited about reading something that is going to make them feel guilty. They tend to throw away items they believe have to do with religion and the church. Your pamphlet should not come across as spiritual or churchy at first.

Use a people format. Make your pamphlet a people pamphlet. Have pictures and symbols that relate to life. Use art work that will draw people to the interior of the pamphlet. Don't use pictures that are outdated.

Remember the major part of the pamphlet should have to do with the benefits and the value of active Sunday School attendance. Satisfied-customer testimonies would be effective in the benefits section.

You should always list the time of your Sunday School and your worship. Don't put all twenty-six opportunities of the week or all fifteen programs in your brochure. If your church changes times often, you may want to leave an open spot in the brochure where you can "rubber stamp" the times a few at a time.

Always include the location of your church in your brochure. Seldom will you find an advertiser telling people how wonderful a product is and then neglecting to tell them where to get it. If your product is worth getting, tell people-where they can get it. Give them good directions and provide a map in the pamphlet if at all possible.

Your pamphlet should be full of pictures and have a lot of white space. This can be done if you choose your words carefully. Pamphlets that are full of text often turn a reader off. Since fewer and fewer people like to read, let's don't demand they read so much to get our message. Have someone edit your pamphlet to reduce wordiness. Use good pictures. A certain percentage of the public cannot read. Would your pamphlet convey a positive message about the Sunday School and your church even if someone couldn't read a word of it?

Imagine this sequence of events. A new family moves into the community fairly close to your church. The family is unchurched and hasn't attended church in a long, long time. Someone visits in the home after seeing the moving van and leaves an invitation to church, along with the church's brochure. During an evening after unpacking many boxes, a tired mom and dad sit down and pick up the brochure and begin to read. They lay it back down, not convinced to attend, but at least they have become aware of the church and that it is reaching out to them.

A week later a teenaged church member gives a teenage member of the new family a youth brochure. It explains the tremendous benefits your church and Sunday School provide for a young person in today's world. It also explains how rewarding it is to be part of an active Bible study class. The teenager comes home and shows the pamphlet to his parents. They immediately notice that the same church has now made two efforts to reach out to them. They begin to realize that the church is serious about drawing them into the fellowship. They have never been invited with so much enthusiasm before.

About two weeks later, two teachers from the children's department of the church drop by to visit the family. (They were told by the first visitor that the family had some children.) After visiting for only a few minutes they say good-bye but leave with the family a pamphlet designed for children. It includes a section (pointed out by the teachers) which is addressed to the parents. This section shares the benefits of having the children in Sunday School. (We've talked about these, remember?) Mom and dad read this pamphlet and notice the tremendous benefits of raising children in the context of the church. They decide right then and there that it is worth their while to visit the church. They want to see if the entire church is as positive and as sincerely interested in them as all these visitors and pamphlets have implied.

This scenario might be repeated thousands of times if we took the time to design brochures and pamphlets in several different areas. People would get the idea that we were serious about the benefits and the values of the Sunday School. The lack of this might be giving them another message.

Carryout Classes

We live in a carryout society today. It used to be that about the only thing that was brought to your house was the paper and the mail. Now you can get everything delivered, from pizza to steak. Everything from videos to a hundred different magazines can be brought to your door. I even noticed the other day that some doctors were beginning to make home visits again. It seems that our society is turning to convenience. More importantly, the public is used to the product being brought to them. I am not suggesting that we change the way we do church so much that no one comes to church anymore. I am suggesting that there are some individuals that can be reached if we would be a little bit more servant minded in the delivery of our product.

Remember when we discussed having different kinds of packaging—different times and different places? Well let's now think about the option of packaging our product in a carryout box.

We know that approximately 20 percent of the public cannot, not will not, come to your church on Sunday morning. Some of these individuals work at jobs they cannot give up. Some of them are ill and their illness keeps them from being involved in the gathering together of the church. Others simply cannot come because of age.

There is also a group of unchurched that cannot come to your church because of shyness. We sometimes piously say that people ought to get over their shyness but several studies I read recently helped me to understand that approximately 10 to 15 percent of the adult population is handicapped by shyness to some degree. Some cases are extreme. These people cannot ask directions or go out in public. Others have some lesser degree of shyness. It may simply be that they feel uncomfortable in a crowd or they feel a little bit out of place in new surroundings. Whatever the reason, shyness may be keeping thousands of people from not only hearing the gospel but participating in the Bible study program of a church.

When we think about those who work on Sunday we often piously say, "Well they should give up that job." I don't believe that is realistic. Somehow I feel, if we called the fire department on Sunday morning and no one was there because everyone had decided to go to church, we would not be too pleased. If we had a wreck on the way to church and there were no police officers to come to our aid, we might be a little bit perturbed. If on the way home from church (even though we say we should not encourage people to work on Sunday), we might not like it if we couldn't get a loaf of bread to make sandwiches for Sunday lunch.

Whether we like it or not, Sunday has become in many ways like any other day and there are a thousand and one different things that people do on Sunday other than go to church. Many of these things have to do with work. We may think that if everybody loved Jesus enough they would quit their job and come to church. I'm not sure that is the way Jesus would approach it. If people can't come to you to receive the gospel, the way I understand the ministry and lifestyle of Jesus, I think He would tell us to carry the gospel to them. Let's think about some ways that we could carry out the Bible study program of our church. Let me offer some versions of *Carryout Sunday School.*

Many churches have offered what is called *homebound* involvement. This is an excellent program whatever form it takes. It is one person carrying the Sunday School lesson to another. I think the program works best when one person, on a regular basis, visits a homebound person and summarizes the lesson in his own words. It doesn't have to be forty-five minutes of in-depth Bible study. He or she shares what the lesson said to his or her heart. The person who receives the Sunday School lesson in this form is counted as a part of the Sunday School program in the homebound department or class. This experience helps elderly and ill people experience the joy of feeling somebody cares about them. It says a lot about a church and a Sunday School class when they are willing to reach out and be servants to these who cannot come. It may be that this homebound ministry could involve some of those individuals who work on Sunday or who don't come because of shyness. Imagine whatwe could do if enough of our Sunday School members would care enough to take what they receive on Sunday morning, summarize it, and then share it with another individual on a regular basis during the week!

Another version of the carryout Sunday School would be the *cassette class.* We have for a long time taped sermons and taken them to people who are sick or elderly, people who couldn't come to the church. Why not do it for the unchurched also? I had an experience in my last pastorate where I had tried to reach a mechanic for several months. I just couldn't get him to become a Christian or even come to church. After I heard a little bit about the shy handicap some people have, I wondered if he would respond if I offered to provide the Bible study without him having to come to the church.

One day I simply stopped in at the service station where he worked. I asked him, "If I tape the Sunday School lesson and bring it to you would you listen to it?" He smiled and said, "Sure, I'll listen to it while I work on the cars here at the garage." It was that easy. I thought about having one of my Sunday School classes taped. I realized that might make the teacher and even the class a little uncomfortable. So I decided it was worth my time to simply summarize the very best of the Sunday School lesson each week and put it on a cassette . So, once a week I would look over the Sunday School lesson (I always did anyhow), and I would share about twenty minutes of the best that the lesson contained. Every week I would drop the tape off, and he would take it and smile. Every week I would pick up the one I left the week before, and I would ask him if he had listened to it, and he would say that he had. I hope all over the country we might begin to try a carryout version of the cassette class and take the Sunday School lesson to thousands of people who are unchurched.

Another version of the carryout Sunday School would be a *Correspondence Class.* There are several possibilities for a class that involves people who like to do home study. It might be that a church could offer a correspondence Sunday School Bible study. Perhaps we will see literature that is provided for home Bible study through Sunday School. I think it would be worth preparing the material even if we have to do it ourselves. A simple Bible study could be mailed to those who cannot attend the Sunday School class. This sheet could give them Scripture to read or maybe even have the Scripture in it. It could guide them through the study and ask questions that they would answer based on the Scripture. If they were to fill out the responses and mail the correspondence back to the church, they would be counted present in the correspondence Sunday School class.

Some people ask, "Why offer all of these different ways. Why don't we just let people come to the church?" Again, I am trying to impress upon us that 20 percent cannot come to the church. Even for those who will not come for some reason, why should we not make a way for them to experience the Word of God in their lives? It seems to me that we ought to use every possible tool, give them every possible opportunity to have the Word of God touch their lives. I have long given up on the notion that it is only Sunday School if you do it on Sunday and in the church. If we don't take our blinders off and begin to do some things differently, we may lose our chance to reach the world we are trying to reach. Somehow, I feel like Jesus would tell us to open our eyes and throw out our nets in a little different way.

Another kind of carryout Sunday School class would be a *video class.* I read the other day that almost 90 percent of the homes in America have a VCR. Isn't that amazing? Ninety percent of the homes in America have a VCR and few churches have any VCR ministry. How can we overlook something so basic? Why do we not tape a twenty-minute class and have it delivered, picked up, or mailed to individuals who are geared so much to the video generation? Now, I am not suggesting we offer this to everybody and have hundreds of videos going out every week, although that would not be the most terrible thing in the world. I believe this kind of class could be and should be offered to those we have been unable to reach with all of the other strategies we have at our disposal.

If we fail to reach an individual using all of the other alternatives, then maybe we should open other doors of opportunity and response. I am being a little untrue to myself. In my heart I really feel we ought to offer everyone more choices as to how they might become involved in Sunday School. I do believe most people enjoy the experience of studying the Bible with small groups. I also believe that Sunday School, as I know and love it, is still the best option. But, I believe we are missing lots of people who will not respond to the invitation to come down to the church on Sunday morning. A video class is not out of the range of possibilities as to how God would have us to reach people. *Think and pray about it!*

Before I leave this section I want to say one other word about those who are handicapped by shyness. I have talked about our need to reach out to these individuals through carryout classes. But I think I must speak a word about how we respond to this type of handicap, even inside the walls of our churches.

Wherever I have gone I have found some degree of resistance to any idea of making it easier for an individual to penetrate the life of the church. We seem to want to make it as difficult as possible, to make a person prove how sincere he or she is about coming into the life of the church and becoming a follower of Jesus Christ. Sometimes I feel we forget that people are babes in Christ even after they are born of the Spirit of God. We seem to expect so much more out of individuals than even Jesus did. Individuals that are handicapped by shyness will have problems coming into our churches for Bible study. We tend to want to recognize them in every possible way. We need to be sensitive to the fact that some people are simply embarrassed to be recognized in any way. Maybe we need to find ways of recognizing our visitors that don't put them on a pedestal, make them raise their hand, or force them to sit down or stand up when everyone else does the opposite. I guess what I am looking for is a strategy by which people can be recognized if they choose to. Somehow I feel that if we offer people enough incentive they might overcome whatever degree of shyness they have to ask for a special brochure telling them about the benefits and the program of the church.

One other thing. The idea of asking every person to come to the front of the church to join the church seems to be, in my estimation, a little bit hard on some people. I remember a man whom I led to Christ in one of my pastorates. He was on his deathbed. After he had received Christ, I presented him to the church for membership, even though he wasn't present. The great majority of the church welcomed him into the church fellowship and didn't mind saying that he was a member of the church when he died only a few days later. But there were still some who said we couldn't say he was a member of the church because he never came and presented himself before the church for membership. It breaks my heart that we are not more sensitive to the special needs of some individuals. It seems to me, when Jesus said that we must be willing to openly confess Him before men, He had in mind far more than walking down to the front of the church. I have never believed that walking to the front of the church saved anybody. Acceptance of the Lord Jesus Christ into a person's life as Savior and Lord brings that person into the kingdom of God. That is done whether a person is standing in the pew or kneeling at the front of the church. Is it possible that we might need to rethink the fact that there are some people who we need to present to the church without asking that they take that long walk to the front?

I remember one man whom I had tried to encourage to come into the church for many months. One day out of pure frustration, trying to find out what was keeping this man back, I asked him if he would join the church if I could present him without his coming to the front. He grinned and said, "Why, of course, that would be just fine." No hesitation whatsoever. I never did ask him about it, but somehow I feel that he would have resisted joining the church for the rest of his life if it meant having to walk down to the front and stand before 400 people in that congregation. I presented him to the church and I said that he was sitting on a pew near the back. I ask him to simply raise his hand so folks could see who he was. There was a motion that receive him and they graciously did. I remember in the weeks to come I received a lot of criticism by some that said, "That is just not the way we do it; you have to come to the front of the church to join."

Well, I am not so sure. I never really felt bad about letting this man become a part of my church family without walking to the front. He was a Christian; I had no doubt about that. He wanted to join our church. I had no doubt about that. And, he joined without walking to the front. I have no doubt about that. So, I am wondering if we might need to offer folks alternative ways to become part of the church family. I still think the best way to join a church is to come down to the front and share this most important decision with the pastor. But, I somehow feel that those who are handicapped by shyness or some other problem should be at least offered an alternative method. If a man had no legs, I am sure we would find a way to get him down to the front. But sometimes I ask myself, why? Can you tell me?

Now let's talk about another marketing tool available to the church.

Church Signs

The importance of church signs cannot be overemphasized. Church signs become a contact point for all of your target audiences. Church signs, used in the correct way, will address every person in every target audience. We have learned that the number of contacts directly affects the response you can expect in attendance. One of the many ways to make contact is through the use of an effective church sign.

Church signs also are tremendous image makers. Your church sign creates in the mind of the viewer an image of what your church is like. Every church has an image. The image may be bad or it may be good. A church's image may simply be neutral. The use of your church signs will help you make sure that your church's image is positive.

Making the Most of Church Signs

Too many churches have no sign at all, or they have neglected the sign that they have. In many cases the church sign they used to have is lying in tall grass or simply faded out of existence. It seems like nobody cares whether the church sign can be read or not. I believe the problem is those who attend the church don't notice that the sign is either in disrepair or totally gone. If your church sign was removed next Saturday would anybody notice on Sunday? The key to a good sign is that it be so effectively used that people take notice of it on a regular basis. If your sign is hanging by one chain, is so faded it is hard to read, or has the name of the pastor that left two years ago still on it, your church sign needs some work.

Some churches have great signs which are either unused, misused, confusing, or wasted. Hundreds, even thousands of dollars have been spent, but the sign has since been ignored. In some cases, rather than ignoring the sign, we have put someone in charge of the sign who has no concept of how it should be used. I often drive by churches where beautiful lighted signs using removable lettering have been erected. The only problem is there are no removable letters on the sign! A big empty space glares out at the community as if to say, "We haven't got anything to say this week." Or, maybe no one could think of anything to say this week. Don't be guilty of investing thousands of dollars in a sign that you will simply neglect. (Spend the thousands and *use the sign!*)

Some signs are misused. By this I mean that space on a sign is valuable. To use the space in an ineffective way is to misuse the sign. For example, putting the name of your pastor on the sign has very little effect other than to boost the ego of the pastor. That's not altogether bad. By having been a pastor for many years I know there is tremendous value in having your ego boosted. There are times when that church sign is about the only thing that you have going for you. This space would probably be better used to put the simple, "Everyone Welcome," or to place the times of your morning gatherings, or to put some image-enhancing slogan. Unless your pastor has a "household" name, it won't do much good just to have his name on the church sign.

Sometimes what is put on church signs is confusing. Have you read what is being put on many lighted-letter signs today? There must be a book somewhere that contains all of the crazy things you can put on a church sign and it must have sold a million copies. Sometimes I have actually called a

118

church to ask what their sign meant. It is important, if you are going to use a removable letter sign and give a message each week, that you stand a half a block away and read the sign yourself. Ask yourself, "What does this mean to a person who seldom attends church?" The person in charge of the sign, usually this should be the pastor or another member of the church staff, should ask each time the sign is changed, "What would I say to thousands of people if I had the chance to say one thing to them?" There are thousands of ways to say it. Your church sign gives you an opportunity to say it fifty-two different ways every year.

If the church is involved in a strategy to market the Sunday School, it would be wise to look for ways to use church signs to do so, whether it is the sign in front of your church or a special sign for the Sunday School. (Oh, we never thought about that!) Or, use the directional signs around the community, or more signs around your church building to make your Sunday School experience more user friendly. It is possible on these signs to help people understand that Sunday School is not just for kids, or that Sunday School is all about understanding the Bible, or that Sunday School can help a person live forever.

Types of Church Signs

There are all types of church signs. First, and probably most used, is the sign in front of the church building itself. This sign normally contains the name of the church, probably when it was organized, and maybe the name of the pastor.

Another type is the sign used to direct people to your church from around the community. These are called directional signs. You don't find many of these signs today but those churches that are using them are usually the growing churches.

Another type of sign that can be utilized around your church is welcome signs. These might include signs about visitors' parking, a sign telling visitors that there is a weather canopy if it is raining, a sign telling visitors which entrance to enter, a sign telling visitors where the nursery can be found, signs helping the visitor find the worship center, and other signs making the church "user friendly." We will address each of these in order.

Let's think for a moment about directional signs around the community. These signs are normally small and are placed at specific intersections which will move people in the direction of the church. Too often churches have no directional signs. In other cases directional signs were erected years ago and have been forgotten. Most of the directional signs you find around communities are old, faded, fallen down, or grown over. Signs which are in disrepair would be better removed. They create a negative image in the minds of the unchurched, before they ever get to the church. Even worse, the negative image is created in the mind of every person that drives by that particular sign.

Is it too much to ask that someone be put in charge of keeping these directional signs in good condition? Consider this. When you are erecting new directional signs or refacing older signs, use the sign for more than just directional purposes. The creative use of color, size, shape, and the message contained can help create a positive image of your church. It doesn't take much more on a directional sign to say something positive about your church. It might be a simple slogan, such as, "The Friendly Place," "The People Place," or "We Welcome You." In some way on the sign say something that creates a good feeling in the mind of the person reading the sign. It is true that it is becoming more difficult to put directional signs up. City ordinances and property restrictions are making it more difficult. But the church has been fighting "restrictions" since the first century (and has always found a way). Don't let a little difficulty cause you to back away and do nothing. There are places to put these signs and it is worth the trouble.

Another type of sign is the on-site sign—those inside your church property. These signs can begin at the entrance to your parking lot and not end until a person is actually seated in a Sunday School class. Do you have signs telling people where to park? By that I mean, do they know where the handicap spaces are? Do they know where to find visitors parking? Do they know if there is a weather canopy for their use? Do they know the entrance closest to the nursery? Do they know which entrance visitors are encouraged to use? Do they know they are welcome? As I travel around, I notice that some churches say nothing before people come in the back door and others have said a lot. I can remember churches with signs at the beginning of the parking lot telling people they were welcome and that visitors' parking has been provided. I remember signs telling folks that there is a place where they can unload in rainy weather and let their family out without getting soaking wet. I can remember walking down a sidewalk and being told three or four times before I got to the first door that the church was glad that I had decided to come and that they were looking forward to getting to know me. I can remember walking into a church door feeling that I was welcome before the first person said the first word to me. It doesn't take much money to begin to communicate through "on-site signs." Let's make a list of all of the possibilities of signs that you could have on your church property that would enhance the image of your church and make it more user friendly.

1. Welcome signs at the entrances of your parking lot.
2. An attractive well-lighted church sign

121

3. Visitors parking signs at eye level.
4. Handicap parking signs at eye level.
5. Weather canopy signs at the entrance
6. Welcome signs over every entrance
7. Welcome signs painted on the sidewalks as you come in.
8. Signs of welcome in church hallways.
9. Welcome signs in individual classrooms.
10. Rest room directional signs.
11. Rest room location signs extending over the door.

Are there other signs that would make your church more appealing and user friendly?

In one church where we had used all of this sign strategy we heard people say, "I never felt so welcome in a church." They went on to say that they had felt welcome before anyone said the first word to them. This was accomplished through the use of an effective church sign strategy.

Billboards

Billboards are among the most expensive tools available to the church. Along with television, they will use a lot of your advertising and marketing resources. This is not to say that you should not use them. These tools are extremely effective. As the church builds its advertising or marketing budget, it will find itself within a period of years having enough money to use more expensive tools. One of the objectives of your marketing strategy should be to increase the amount you use every year until you are able to use a good variety of marketing tools, including those that are more expensive.

The cost of billboards is hard to nail down. Different cities and communities are different markets. Therefore, the cost will be determined by supply and demand. Second, billboard costs continue to change. In 1990 in a medium-sized city the average billboard costs $500 for one month. The same billboard for six months would costs between $800 and $1,000. You could get eight billboards for one month for about $3,000. The wise choice as you develop your marketing strategy would be to inquire about the present cost of billboards in your community.

Billboards are more effective in some cities and areas than in others. For example, one billboard in a large city has little impact. One billboard in a small community where 90 percent of the community drives by it at least once or twice a month would have major impact. It is ironic that those who would benefit most by billboards because they live in small communities are the least able to afford them. This is why even small churches should begin building their advertising budget and continue to build it until they are able to do some of the things that would impact their community the greatest.

Placement of billboards is extremely important. One church placed its billboard only a block from the front door of its church facing a major traffic artery. This gave additional visibility to the church with people who were traveling the roads in that part of town. They also used this billboard to create a positive image about the church. Creative ads and content are easy to come by if you will brainstorm what you would say to people if you could say it to thousands every day. Ad agencies are also available at a cost to help you think about the content of your billboard.

Think about the target audience. Is there a specific age group? Or is your billboard to be used to attract all ages and all types of people? Once you determine whom you are trying to attract, design your content to attract that particular audience. In my opinion, content of billboards should attract the larger target audience. Use your billboard to create a positive image about who your church really is. Project a servant image on your billboard. Tell those that read your billboard what your church will do for them. I don't believe it does a lot of good to tell the whole community that your church is growing. Most of the folks who don't attend church could care less that your church is growing and may not be attracted to success measured in terms of numbers. Better yet, tell them why your church is growing. Tell them what your church can do for them. Tell them "Why" they ought to invest the time and energy to be in your church.

Another type of billboard is the community billboard or poster. In many communities there are opportunities for small signs or smaller billboards in places like ballparks, community parks, and on city streets. Opportunities are available to make your church visible on bus benches, grocery store carts, movie screens, and the list goes on. Advertisers are finding new ways to advertise, and the church should constantly be alert to the opportunities the industry makes available. This is why it is vitally important for a church to have a person or a group of persons responsible for continually evaluating the marketing strategy. Billboards and community billboards can be effectively used to communicate the message that you wish to communicate to your target audiences. Don't stop increasing your marketing budget until you are able to utilize these tools from time to time.

Door Hangers

Door hangers have been around for a long time. I remember as a young boy finding a door hanger on my front door fairly often. Some communities have passed ordinances that keep churches and businesses from using door hangers. If this is not the case in your community, this is one of the tools available to your church for your marketing strategy. A door hanger is simply a small cardboard piece that is attached to the doorknob of all of the homes in a particular area. One of the advantages of this type of marketing tool is its low cost. It is possible to get across the message through the use of a door hanger. Young people or other particular groups in your church can put door hangers out in a target area on a Saturday morning or one night during the week. This does not require that you ring the doorbell or interrupt the people who live in the residence. Normally, they will see the door hanger within a day or so. Remember to place the door hanger at the door closest to the cars.

Door hangers should be well designed. Make good use of the limited space. Tell the benefits and values of attending the Sunday School. Remember the possible use of satisfied customers testimonies. Don't list every activity, but simply the Sunday morning opportunities. Consider targeting particular areas, such as singles' apartments with a door hanger that talks about opportunities your church makes available to singles. An area where young couples live could be targeted with a door hanger about your children's ministry or your day-care program, and so forth.

Be careful and ask yourself, "Do you want to date your door hanger?" Often half of your door hangers will be used only to find the other half is outdated within a week or two. If you are promoting a particular event with your door hanger that is one thing. But if you are printing thousands of door hangers featuring the benefits and values or a particular program (Sunday School), don't date it by putting a picture of your pastor on it or by talking about a particular event that will take place in the near future. Keep your content such that it would be true months or even a year into the future.

Bumper Stickers

Bumper stickers are another option for your marketing strategy. They are effective in increasing the number of contacts made by the church and giving the church more visibility. Although many people do not like bumper stickers, the number of people who use them make it possible for your church to become visible all over the community in an inexpensive way. Bumper stickers range from $1 to $5 each, depending on the size and quality. One of the objections to bumper stickers in the past is that it is hard to remove them. New bumper stickers have been designed so they are easy to remove.

The objective of a bumper sticker is to make your church more visible in your community. Think about it—a sign on a car travels the streets of your city every day. Multiply that by dozens or even hundreds and you see the tremendous value of bumper stickers. If at every turn, people see the name of your church being displayed, they begin to notice the large number of "satisfied customers" who enjoy the benefits of your Sunday School and church. There is a powerful message there. The impact of bumper stickers may be greatest on those looking for a church already. But we cannot minimize the power of a large number of bumper stickers to speak to the unchurched. Consider what would happen if you were able to gather every Christian in your city in one place at one time. I am sure the crowd would be impressive. If only 20 to 30 percent of your community attends church, it is still an impressive sight. If bumper stickers are used it has a similar impact. Everywhere people go they see other people who are actively involved in a church.

If you are using bumper stickers to market your Sunday

School, you will want to create, as we have with other marketing tools, a positive image of the Sunday School experience. Space will limit what you can say on your bumper sticker but it can be effectively done. The simple statement, "Sunday School is not just for kids at First Church," or "I learned to understand the Bible at First Church," or just the simple words, "I attend Bible study at First Church," is an effective way to use your satisfied customers as they drive around your city.

One thing that I noticed in my use of these marketing tools in the local church has been the boost in the self-image of the church family and in the church leadership itself. There is a certain amount of pride in seeing your name on anything. Those that attend your church regularly get a certain "lift" when they see the name of their church all over the city. As active church members see the name of their church more and more often, there seems to be an increased pride in what their church stands for and in their own personal commitment to their church.

Telemarketing

As we discuss this area of our marketing strategy, we must realize there are good and bad aspects about using this tool. Telemarketing is the communication of your marketing message through the telephone. Telecommunication is based on the theory of large numbers. By this we mean, if you call enough people and ask a specific action out of those people, a small percentage of those people will respond. For example, if you call 20,000 people you could expect 2,000 to allow their names to be put on a mailing list to receive further information. Of that 2,000 you might expect 200 to respond in some specific way to attend your church.

Let's think about some negative sides of telemarketing. Most people say that telemarketing will not work because people are tired of businesses calling them with a sales pitch. This might be true. It even might be true that telemarketing can have some negative impact on the general community. Although we might irritate some people by calling them, they will, without a doubt, get the message that the church is still out there and still cares enough about them to make the effort. The negative impact of bothering someone might be akin to the New Testament experience of the church. Remember it said in the Book of Acts, "And they troubled the people and the rulers of the city when they heard these things" (17:8). Remember, it also said in verse 6 that they turned their world upside down. Somehow, I get the idea that the New Testament church did not mind bothering people. It may be that we have become a little too careful. It may be that a little "annoying" is not all bad. I believe that telemarketing has a place in the overall strategy of marketing the Sunday School and the church. Done in a tactful way and with some discretion, it can be effectively used.

Telemarketing is not just for the unchurched. Telemarketing can be used as a powerful tool to reach several of your target audiences inside the church. Think about the possibilities of using the telephone to contact all of your inactive members. You could also use this kind of strategy to target all of those who attend your worship service but who do not attend Sunday School. Keep in mind the tremendous value of a telephone call on a Saturday night preceding a high attendance day.

Keep in mind the powerful use of satisfied-customer testimonies in your use of telemarketing. Build around the value, benefits, and personal testimony of a satisfied customer. If you are promoting a high-attendance day this coming Sunday, use a satisfied customer and focus on the benefits rather than just trying to get someone to help you reach your goal.

Most telemarketing programs use far more than just the telephone. They involve preparation time which includes tremendous prayer involvement. Remember what we have said, nothing we do will be effective without the power of the Holy Spirit, and we can do nothing without a strategy of prayer. These programs also have follow-up through letters and other marketing tools. Follow-up is as important as the phone calls themselves. If you are to expect the average return of 1 to 2 percent of your total calls you must be serious about follow-up work that is involved. Just as with direct mail, repetition is important in your contact process. If follow-up is neglected, response will fall drastically.

One other word about the telemarketing process. If a phone bank is used, by that I mean many people are involved in the phoning of a large number of your target audience; there is an added benefit that comes from involving so many people in an evangelistic outreach effort. This involvement has potential to bring revival and renewal to the lives of many in your church. For others, it will heighten the awareness that your church exists. I cannot say enough about the importance of your church being involved in any of the marketing tools because of the impact that it will have on the active church family itself. Telemarketing is one of the many tools God has placed at our disposal that the early church would have given anything to possess.

Summary

With so many possibilities for marketing the Sunday School, it becomes apparent that someone or some group needs to plan and implement the marketing strategy. It is also apparent why a yearly calendar or plan is needed. You can't do all this at once. Plan your usage each year and begin to multiply the different tools that you are using. Increase your budget and your activity every year and in five years you will not believe the difference it has made, not only in your church itself, but in the impact your church is having on the community around it. There are additional marketing tools that I have not mentioned in this book. Many marketing tools are yet to be discovered or invented. The creative changes that the use of these tools will generate will help your church be on the cutting edge of new strategies in the future. Maybe your church will develop yet another way to communicate the gospel and the value of attending the Sunday School and church for others to use.

6

The Content of Your Marketing Message

The content of your marketing message is critical. This chapter will deal with what you say and how you say it. We will touch on all three types of advertising: awareness, selection, and maintenance. We will talk about the fact that different content for different target audiences is essential. We will also look at how your ad ideas should be shaped by your content.

As we think about content, let's think first about addressing needs. Remember your marketing strategy is to surface needs that already exist in the life of the individual. It may even be said that we can create need. By that I mean creating or enhancing a need that would seldom be recognized by anyone. People may not know they have a need to understand the Bible until we explain the tremendous value of doing so. In essence, your marketing strategy can create primary need by the surfacing of secondary needs. Address those needs that you believe exist or could exist in the lives of those you are trying to reach.

Talk about benefits. Remember that guilt does not work today. Rather than telling people how bad they are for not attending your Sunday School, explain the benefits they will receive if they do attend your Sunday School. If a group brainstorms about the benefits involved in Sunday School attendance, I am convinced they will be amazed at how

60544)

many benefits surface. Let's think about a few of the benefits that can be gained by regular attendance in Sunday School.

1. Learn how to live forever (self-preservation).
2. New friends.
3. Learn the meaning of Bible passages.
4. Understand the meaning of life.
5. Gain support during the crises of life.
6. Be a better husband or wife.
7. Help keep your children off drugs.
8. Teach your family how to communicate better.
9. Help children to respect and obey parents.
10. Inner peace.
11. Satisfaction with life.
12. Hope for tomorrow.
13. The power to change your life.
14. Someone who can love you.
15. Somebody you can love.
16. Something to look forward to (heaven).

And on and on the list can go. What benefits would you add to the list?

Most people look at advertising as a positive tool, not only for the marketer, but also for the consumer. It gives them information about products that are available and the benefits of using those products. This means that when you consider the content of your marketing strategy, you should seek to inform the public about the benefits of the Sunday School experience. Your marketing strategy involves informing the public about who you are and what you are as the church. Second, your information should include a list of the benefits that will be received from the Bible study program (the product).

Another important point about content is that we consider the use of humor. Recent surveys show that those who view advertising of any type respond more positively if the advertising makes them laugh. It may be that some amount of humor can be used in the marketing process for the church and the Sunday School. In some of the prepared ads, companies do involve the use of humor in their church advertising.

Repetition is another important factor as we consider the content of our ads. Realize that 60 percent of everything you learn today you will forget in twenty-four hours. That is heartbreaking to some of us who preach and teach, but it is reality. This forgetfulness factor makes it imperative that we use repetition. For example, the same ad can be run several times over a period of time. Also, ads must be run several times to receive the maximum benefit. This means your ad should be short enough to not drain your financial resources and allow you to use the ad more often. Of course, the ideal is to have large ads and enough financial resources to use repetition even with the large ads.

As you consider the content of your marketing strategy, here are some questions you need to ask yourself. *Is it clear?* By that we mean, can it be understood by just about anyone? We have heard a lot about the reading skills of the public. It is important that you write clearly enough that anyone can understand the message you are presenting. Next question?

Is it believable; is it true? It is important that the church have the highest regard for "Truth in advertising." Your advertising content must be true. It should be worded in such a way that it is believable. Be careful that you don't open yourself up to accusations of false advertising. Don't promise things you cannot deliver. You have enough that you can deliver; tell them about that.

THE CONTENT OF YOUR MARKETING MESSAGE

Is it too wordy? Say what you want to say in the shortest amount of space. Use the fewest words possible. Some say that if you involve people in your ad through your headline they will read any amount of copy. I think both are true. So, involve them through the headline so that they will read any number of words you put in the ad. Yet, be conscious of the fact that you are in danger of losing your reader if you are too wordy. Therefore, edit, edit, edit, and then edit again. Choosing your words carefully so that finally your ad is the best possible presentation with the fewest possible words. This takes work!

Does the headline grab you? Every ad has a headline. It is the first thing people hear or see. The question you must ask is, "would this headline get my attention if I were in the target audience?" If you believe it wouldn't, change it. In a recent meeting of our public-relations committee, we spent nearly two hours selecting about two dozen words for an ad. Keep improving that headline until you get the best possible response out of it. Your headline should contain the main point of what you are trying to say or at least draw people into that main point. The rest of your ad is follow-up. This is the proof of the evidence of the main point. Don't present the proof and evidence first. Start out with your main point and follow up with supporting material.

Choose *action verbs* and use few adjectives. Use the simplest words possible; these are not normally the first words you think of. Read your copy again and again asking yourself, "Is there a *simpler word* that can be used to say the same thing even better?" Avoid long words and remember that the average person reads on a fifth-to sixth-grade level. Keep your *sentences short.* I have found that I am terrible about using super long sentences. My average sentence can usually be broken down into three shorter sentences. I'm getting the knack of it. Give it a try!

Are there misspelled words? One of the most distracting things about any type of printed ad is misspelled words. I am not a good speller and it is essential that two or three other people read my material before it goes to press. Whatever you are working on, however well you think you have "spelled" everything, ask a second person to proofread your material. It is best if two other people read the same ad looking specifically for misspelled words.

Are there *overworked words?* Every generation finds some words so attractive that they use them over and over. These words lose their impact. Look at the wording in your ads and ask yourself if a word has lost its impact and if there is another word which would communicate your message more powerfully.

Are there *pictures?* A picture is worth a thousand words. Not only do pictures help reinforce what you are trying to say, oftentimes they become the power behind the message itself. Ask yourself two important questions. *Are the pictures I am using the most effective pictures that could be used? Second, are there pictures I could use which I have not yet considered?* Your choice of pictures should take into account copyright problems. But there are numbers of pictures available. Artwork is available for computers and there are art books by the thousands, especially designed pictures that can be used for publication. Purchase them or get acquainted with someone who has these resources at their disposal.

Have we included *what, when, where, what time, how, how much it will cost, and what are the benefits?* All of these things should be in your ad, if possible. How often I have prepared an ad and sent it to press when I realized I omitted the event's time, address, or cost. I now proofread every ad and all the publicity with a list of these items nearby.

It is important to understand that many people do not know that the church is free. Most church activities are free.

THE CONTENT OF YOUR MARKETING MESSAGE

I have actually met people who think the church assesses the amount people pay each week. Surveys show readers don't trust advertising that does not include the cost. Therefore, if your price is nominal or free, be sure and say so. This can be done in tactful ways in church advertising. But don't assume that everybody understands.

Have you used *questions?* Recent studies show one of the most popular ways to get attention is to ask questions. Questions are more powerful than an exclamation mark. Questions draw your target audience into the communication process. ("Don't you think so?") Asking a question demands some type of response. This causes your target audience to think about the ad or at least the question. This often will draw them into the content of the ad.

Have I used a *contact mechanism?* Every ad should ask your target audience to do something, and you need to be specific about what you are asking them to do. You may want them to call you for further information. You may ask them to send in a response coupon for free material or even a free gift. You may have given them a contact mechanism which simply offers to be available to them anytime just to talk. I was so pleased to hear some of the newest ads being written for churches included the closing phrase, "Call us at (phone number) for further information or just to talk." This contact mechanism provides not only a way of response but also presents a positive servant attitude of the church.

Are you using *words that communicate well?* Certain words communicate well with the church community but do not communicate well at all with the unchurched community. Think about who your target audience is every time you do a new ad. If your target audience understands church terminology then use it. But if your target audience does not understand the theological and church words that are used so often, then find better words that communicate more effectively. I remember meeting with a group of about a dozen laypersons for over twelve weeks discussing the content of one pamphlet. We often argued about whether certain words communicated. It was surprising that many of the words we used so frequently inside the church have either no meaning or confusing meanings outside the church. Take time to listen to your ads through the ears of the unchurched.

Are you using your *slogan or logo?* It is a positive decision for a church to choose a slogan or logo. This slogan or logo creates a positive impression of the church in the mind of the target audience. Oftentimes the slogans that I see for churches are too religious. They talk about the second coming, about a growing church—things that most unchurched could care less about. The wise slogan or logo projects the servant attitude and helps the church communicate to the unbeliever, to the unchurched, what your church can do for them.

Are you *putting down other churches?* Too often we do not realize that we are putting down other churches around us in our ads. This became very clear when we analyzed one of our ads that said, "The Caring People." A concerned member of our committee said the ad sounded like we were saying we were the only caring people around. After much discussion, a simple deletion of the word *the* left the slogan much more positive. "Caring People" simply said that we were some of the caring people and that our church was just one of many who cared. Ask yourself if your advertising tends to put down other churches in your community. If it does, you may be doing positive advertising with some target audiences but cutting your throat with others. If you say that your church is the most exciting church in town or the most loving church in town, you sound like you think every other church in town cares less and is less exciting than you are. This might be true, but to say it in your advertising may hurt you in the long run.

What about *layout?* As you lay out ads for newspaper, magazines, newsletters, and so on, you should consider certain factors. First, consider balance. Balance does not always mean that everything on the page is balanced by something of equal size on the opposite side of the page. That is what I call "real balance." But there is what I call "imagined balance," which is also good. It might involve a small object on the left side of the page which is balanced by a much larger object on the opposite side of the page. Look at your ad as a whole. Does it seem balanced to you?

Is there *motion* in the ad? Does the ad flow from one line to the next line? Are you drawn from one thought into the next thought? This can be done by the way you arrange the ad, the size of your copy, and by the way you position the different elements in your ad.

Do I have enough *white space?* I always want to fill up every available inch of paper. I learned that white space sometimes is more valuable than words. Every ad needs considerable white space. Too much type causes your ad to be too domineering, too threatening.

Is the *main thing emphasized first?* Having a "dominant element" is important. What is the most important thing you want to say? What do you want readers to see first? Give this most important element the highest priority space in your ad. Make it stand out.

What about the *use of color?* We often hear that full color is the best and it probably is. The problem with full color is cost. If you are working with limited funds, two colors may be as effective as a full-color ad. Popular colors change from year to year. One color may be hot now but may leave people cold next year. Talk to advertising people. Many of them will be glad to give you advice.

Because there are so many different factors involved in the layout of printed ads, it is important that you consider getting professional help. A wise church will build its budget year by year until it is able to hire a professional to help with designing ads. Remember this may be some of the most important money your church ever spends.

Conclusion

It is a new day for the church. So many things are changing around us. Our world is different today, and it will continue to change for each new generation. This simply means a new challenge for the church. The church has always existed in a world of change, but it has always met the challenge with resolve. This world of change also becomes the source of new resources. The church has resources at its disposal today that have never been available before. We have been talking about many of those resources in the preceding chapters.

A "Marketing Strategy" is not the total answer to the needs of the church today, but it will give the church new tools to work with as we seek to reach this changing world. We cannot lose sight of the total picture. The most aggressive marketing strategy will not reach our world without the presence of those things that have brought the church this far.

Preaching the gospel is essential to growth of the church. We cannot neglect this and survive. We need to consider all the options for the preaching of the "good news" today.

Worship that takes place in our churches is a vital, indispensable activity of the church. We must continue to make the worship services in our churches an exciting encounter with the living God.

The caring ministry of the church can never be minimized for those who seek to live as Jesus lived. The church must always love people and seek to meet their every need.

Evangelism and missions will never be replaced by anything as the heartbeat of the church. This is the *mission* of the church, and we must resist any attempt to place anything else as the number-one priority in the church.

The Sunday School marketing strategy undergirds all that we do in the church. It becomes one of the vehicles the church uses to "compel them in." It will help us do what our Lord has commissioned us. The Sunday School is still our strongest evangelistic program and can do more to reach our world than we can imagine. Its greatest day yet is still ahead, if the church allows it to adapt to the changing world. Part of this adapting is the addition of the aggressive marketing strategy detailed in this book. The church must stay flexible in its methods. It must add to those proven methods of church growth the newest resources as they become available.

It will not be easy. Satan will do all in his power to keep the church "behind the times" and behind the scenes. He will use anyone who will let him to discourage the use of powerful new tools. The forces of evil will carefully and quietly influence the church to spend its energy and resources on things that have little or no impact on the lost, unchurched world. There will be church fights, dismissed pastors and staff members, and every conceivable problem the evil world can put together. But, the church of Jesus Christ is up to it; we are ready for the final assault on the gates of hell, those gates on which Jesus told us to march in Matthew 16. We march with the power of the Holy Spirit in us, the spiritual needs of our hurting world before us, and the resources and tools to get the work done.

The key is leadership. It has always been the key. The church will not march without an earthly general. I don't fully understand that but God does. He has always sent leaders to the "people of God." *Are you one of these leaders?* It will not be easy but it is necessary! Pastors, staff ministers, and lay leaders alike must break with the traditions of yesterday and do whatever it takes to get the church marching more aggressively. Someone must stand up and lead the church to invest a larger portion of its resources and energies in the march, in the assault on those gates of darkness. If not, the gates of hell will continue to stand in the lives of millions of lost and unchurched people. The gates will not stand against us if we march; but *we must march!*

I choose to end this book with a checklist for the marketing strategy. I have found that it helps me to have a summary of what I read. It helps me put into action what I have read. I hope it will help you. So, tear this book up! Tear the last pages out. Put them on your wall or your mirror; give them to the "person in charge" of your marketing strategy.

Marketing Strategy Checklist and Notes

_____ Pray today about your marketing activity
_____ Make someone responsible for the marketing strategy
_____ Preach about the "reaching-people" priority
_____ List all the "benefits" of Sunday School attendance
_____ List your target audiences
_____ Put together a marketing "calendar of activities"
_____ Budget for the marketing activity
_____ Increase your budget for marketing
_____ Improve the "packaging" of your Sunday School
_____ Building
_____ Grounds
_____ Parking

_____ Friendliness of your people
_____ Welcome center and committee
_____ Remember the three types of church advertising/ use them
_____ Awareness advertising
_____ Selection advertising
_____ Maintenance advertising
_____ Use your satisfied customers
_____ Visitation
_____ Teach them to talk to everyone about church and the benefits of Sunday School
_____ Give them a marketing piece to use
_____ Use them in the pulpit
_____ Put their testimony in your marketing pieces
_____ Use direct mail
_____ Use newspaper ads
_____ Use your church mail out
_____ Make use of your Sunday bulletin
_____ Use radio
_____ Use television
_____ Start port-of-entry classes
_____ Use VBS Family Night to market your Sunday School
_____ Use pulpit spots
_____ Use your wall space and bulletin boards
_____ Produce a Sunday School brochure:
_____ General
_____ Youth
_____ Singles
_____ Senior Adult
_____ Children

Other:_____
_____ Start carryout classes

CONCLUSION

_____ Homebound class
_____ Cassette class
_____ Video class
_____ Correspondence class
_____

Other:_____
_____ Improve your sign strategy
_____ Use door hangers
_____ Use billboards
_____ Use bumper stickers
_____ Use telemarketing
_____ Think of other tools to use in your area
_____ Think about your content

The world is waiting on the church to give them a good reason to attend the Sunday School. Has yours?